LINK
OUT

LINK OUT

HOW TO TURN YOUR NETWORK INTO A CHAIN OF LASTING CONNECTIONS

LESLIE GROSSMAN

WILEY

John Wiley & Sons, Inc.

Cover design: C. Wallace

Published by John Wiley & Sons, Inc., Hoboken, New Jersey.
Published simultaneously in Canada.

Limit of Liability/Disclaimer of Warranty: While the publisher and author have used their best efforts in preparing this book, they make no representations or warranties with the respect to the accuracy or completeness of the contents of this book and specifically disclaim any implied warranties of merchantability or fitness for a particular purpose. No warranty may be created or extended by sales representatives or written sales materials. The advice and strategies contained herein may not be suitable for your situation. You should consult with a professional where appropriate. Neither the publisher nor the author shall be liable for damages arising herefrom.

For general information about our other products and services, please contact our Customer Care Department within the United States at (800) 762-2974, outside the United States at (317) 572-3993 or fax (317) 572-4002.

Wiley publishes in a variety of print and electronic formats and by print-on-demand. Some material included with standard print versions of this book may not be included in e-books or in print-on-demand. If this book refers to media such as a CD or DVD that is not included in the version you purchased, you may download this material at http://booksupport.wiley.com. For more information about Wiley products, visit www.wiley.com.

Library of Congress Cataloging-in-Publication Data:

Grossman, Leslie, 1947-
    Link out: How to Turn Your Network into a Chain of Lasting Connections/Leslie Grossman.
        p.   cm.
    Includes index.
    ISBN: 978-1-118-38058-1 (cloth); ISBN: 978-1-118-42073-7 (ebk);
    ISBN: 978-1-118-41732-4 (ebk); ISBN: 978-1-118-54303-0 (ebk)
      1. Business networks.   2. Strategic alliances (Business)   3. Interpersonal relations.   I. Title.
    HD69.S8G76   2013
    650.1'3—dc23
                                                                        2012038547

Printed in the United States of America
10 9 8 7 6 5 4 3 2 1

This book is dedicated to my mother, Charlotte, and my dad, Jack, who taught me the power of love, mutual support, and connection. If everyone had them as role models, this book would not be necessary.

Contents

Acknowledgments

Writing a book is a lot like having a baby. After you give birth and nurture it, you forget all the pain you experienced in delivering it. Then you decide to do it all over again.

In both cases, I have my husband, Richie, to thank. Thanks to his loving support, patience, and understanding, I completed two books, and, together, we raised two amazing children, Josh and Sara. Watching my kids navigate their own careers—with minimal coaching from me—to become hugely successful on their own was the inspiration for this book. From them I learned that linking out is sometimes in the genes, but most people need to be shown the way.

Which brings me to acknowledging my parents. My dad, Jack, was the ultimate connector. When I was a child I would watch him strike up meaningful conversations with complete strangers, whether we were visiting historic sites like the Gettysburg Battlefield or on a group fishing boat off Bridgeport, CT; wherever he went, he made new friends. My mom, Charlotte, never met a person she didn't want to help. Together, my parents were a power couple of a different kind, connecting with people of all backgrounds, colors, religions, and nationalities, and making a difference in people's lives.

This book would not exist without the mutual collaboration, support, and encouragement of thousands of business owners, professionals, leaders, and students with whom I have connected over the years at conferences, events, associations, and speaking engagements. By getting to know so many of them and learning about their successes and struggles, I was motivated to write *Link Out*. I must single out a few extraordinary people who have been there constantly to advise me, connect me, laugh with me, and give me a hug when I most needed it. I am eternally grateful to Edie Weiner, Debra Duneier, Cary Broussard, Sharon Emek, Marcia Wilson, Richard D'Ambrosio, Ann Stock, Marnie Omanoff, Tony Smith, Judy Faine, Leslie Greene, Sharon Hadary, Judy George, David Leffler, Hiroko Tatebe, Betsy Berkhemer Credaire, Susan Sussman, Runa Magnus, Joan Wangler, and Herb Hellman. Special recognition goes to my dear friend Mary Schnack, who lost her battle with cancer in 2012. Her inspiring life was dedicated to linking out, and paying it forward. Together they showed me the true meaning of the *new* entourage, and I am committed to being there to support them in every way I possibly can.

Thank you to the committed members of the National Association of Women Business Owners (NAWBO), an organization in which mutual support is the unwritten law. At NAWBO I immersed myself in the power of linking out and was rewarded 100 times over with an entourage that spread throughout the United States and across the sea.

I have the utmost appreciation to Andrea March, cofounder (with me) of Women's Leadership Exchange (WLE), and the many women who helped us launch and grow WLE by serving on our advisory board or speaking at our conferences. It was their generosity and friendship that helped me visualize the link out model, and they will be lifelong members of my entourage.

I owe thanks to Stacey Radin, founder of Unleashed, a breakthrough leadership program for middle school girls, who upon hearing my vision connected me with Dr. Thomas Ellett, assistant vice president of Student Affairs at New York University. In true entourage fashion, he introduced me to Robert Caparaz, associate director, and Rebecca Salk, assistant director of NYU's Wasserman Center for Career Development. Thanks to them I began presenting the *new* link out concept to hundreds of students and alumni in workshops. It was their feedback and success that encouraged me to write this book.

I have had the pleasure of working with several corporations that understand the importance of linking out to grow healthy, fulfilled, effective teams and how that comes back in increased revenue and sales. I am especially thankful to corporate leaders like Marilyn Johnson, vice president of market development for IBM, and her successor, Denise Evans; Patti Ross, former executive of IBM's international market development group; Miguel Centeno, managing director, community relations, and Kate Begley, vice president of specialty sales, AETNA; Pernille Spiers Lopez, former CEO/president of IKEA North America; Astrid Oyo, leader of IKEA Business US and Global; Kathy Tague, assistant vice president, sales, and training and development, MetLife; Amy Jo Stark, senior director, Best Buy; Michael Trebony, former director of entrepreneurial initiatives, Best Buy, now at Apple;

Jen Rybar, small business customer team, Best Buy; Julie Gilbert, creator of Best Buy's innovative WOLF program, founder of Wolf Means Business and PreciousStatus; Lisa Galante, senior vice president, sales performance, Capital One Bank; Tom Sclafani, vice president, public affairs, American Express; and Richard Murasso, senior vice president, Signature Bank.

Thanks to John Wiley & Sons, Inc., for publishing *Link Out* so that people everywhere will have the tools to take control of their own futures and never have to feel alone. I particularly want to thank Adrianna Johnson, my editor at Wiley, who was first to realize the value of *Link Out* and whose guidance and suggestions made the book infinitely better. Thanks, also, to Christine Moore, Susan Moran, and other Wiley team members who helped see the manuscript through the publishing process; as well as Peter Knox and Melissa Torra, who have supported me in sharing the link out strategy with the many people who can benefit from it.

Introduction

Most of us learn, during our early years in school, that, in order to succeed in this world, we need to memorize facts and soak information into our brains. The more we know, our teachers told us, the better we will do in this world. The more we learn, the higher our grades will be. We'll get more recommendations from teachers and professors, land better jobs, earn higher salaries, enjoy more success in our careers, and lead happier lives. This seems to be a simple formula, yet, as we all know, it is incredibly complicated, but it is a formula that people followed for many, many years.

However, there's always been a missing link—a substantial one—in our education system. No one teaches us how to *create relationships,* the very thing necessary to ensure that every step in the formula cited earlier works. We need to make connections to other people in order to lead fulfilling lives, personally and professionally.

Of course, most of us know we need each other for love and friendship, but we also need each other for support, advice, and connection. In order for our relationships to thrive, we need to learn how to speak and listen to each other. We must learn civility, generosity, and etiquette. We need to understand how to respect one another. Unfortunately, we are not all born with these attributes or habits, and few children actually learn these things at home from their parents.

Many members of the business world believe we know everything about building relationships. After all, we've developed and used basic networking skills to get to where we are. We know how to exchange business cards, have a brief conversation, and move on quickly to the next person. Does this count as building relationships?

Absolutely not! Think about what typically results from this classic networking: a very tall tower of business cards from people we know little about and most likely will never see again. That's the old school way of making connections, but it simply doesn't work in today's professional world.

Today, people want to do business with people they *trust*. They want to recommend and have a relationship with people they trust. We don't build trust by exchanging business cards and having a three-minute conversation.

Whatever your professional goals are, whether you are looking for customers, a better job, advice, or to meet people who can help you achieve your dreams, you need to know how to build relationships. If you are launching, rebooting, or transitioning your career or business—or you simply want to take your life from point A to point B—strong relationships will get you there. If you analyze the lives of successful leaders, salespeople, entrepreneurs, CEOs, politicians, educators, artists, entertainers—you name it—you can see the ways in which their relationships with others propelled them toward success. Yes, many had raw talent or intelligence; however, without other people to nurture, direct, connect and advise them, talent and intelligence alone will stagnate.

As renowned innovator Steve Jobs said, ". . . great things in business are never done by one person, they're done by a team of people." Each of us needs more of the human element to progress on our journey.

Hundreds of thousands of people felt alone and power-lessness when they lost their jobs or their businesses failed during the recent recession. The ones who had a group of influential people to provide them with morale and business support were likely able to get them through this period with less difficulty. All of us, no matter what our jobs or industries, need this kind of support system. Therefore, my goal in writing this book is to ensure that people in all positions—employees, employers, consultants, business owners, students, or retirees—have the resources available when they need advice, encouragement, or a push in their work and careers. These resources can be at your fingertips when you have an entourage. That is what this book has set out to do: show you how to build your very own entourage of people who support you in the good times and the bad.

The Secret Strategy of Leaders

Have you ever felt stuck in a job you don't like or that frustrates you? Are you in a business that doesn't seem to be going anywhere; or in a career that no longer fulfills? Perhaps worst of all, are you stuck without a job or a source of income? Maybe you are just out of college or grad school and are launching your career, or you want to go back to work after staying home to dedicate yourself to raising your children. You may have been downsized or fired for no good reason or you are in transition. Maybe you run your own small business or you are a consultant, coach, or sales rep and have the job of getting new clients and customers in order to generate revenue.

Like most of us, you need a dependable income. Or maybe the idea of being retired just bores you. I venture to guess that very few people on this planet *haven't* felt stuck at least once (and probably more) in their career. I have experienced this very same feeling myself. So you are not alone by any means.

What if I told you there was a solution to these frustrating and often downright depressing situations? Would you be interested?

Chances are that if you picked up this book in the first place, you answered yes. So welcome aboard! I'm going to teach you the route that successful people, including some of the greatest leaders in the world, have been using for centuries. It's an exciting journey, and if you follow the rules, it promises you a fulfilling life. That's why our greatest leaders—presidents; CEOs; entrepreneurs; millionaires and billionaires; politicians; the most successful people in business, the arts, education; and even those in the nonprofit sector—all follow this map, though they take different paths. Few actually talk about it, and nobody teaches it.

I'm going to share this journey, as I have personally experienced it. It's been the reason that I always make a comeback when things get tough for me, and the reason that I am never alone. I have always had support from a group of incredibly important people—all of whom have my back, no matter what.

4
Link Out

You might wonder why this journey seems to be the secret strategy of so few. Until now, people usually have considered the ability to attract influential people to their private circle an intuitive skill that great leaders and movers and shakers simply possess. Some learned it from mentors who showed them the path by example, but most are just not privy to this strategy—at least not until now.

My Story

The concept behind *Link Out* was unconsciously embedded in my mind at an early age. As a teen, I gravitated to organized groups. I always had a desire to connect with people, so linking out in this way seemed to come naturally to me. Additionally, as the oldest of three children, I was bossy. I liked being in charge. I also liked to help people, however, I also liked to help people and I felt my best when I was being collaborative. I learned this from my parents, who were both dedicated to social change and were active in community organizations.

My dad, Jack, was the owner of a local furniture store in Spry, PA, the president of the local Optimist Club, and a volunteer fireman. My mom gave her time to SCORE (Service Core of Retired Executives) by advising small businesses, was a member of the PTA, and hosted her own local radio show, *Chatter with Charlotte*. I wanted to follow their example and connect with people as soon as there were clubs to join. At 13, I was elected to the student council, and at 14, I joined a national youth organization and eventually became president. I ran for vice president of Dallastown High School. I tried my hand at politics by becoming a teen LBJ (Lyndon

5

Introduction

Baines Johnson) girl during the 1964 presidential campaign, handing out leaflets, making phone calls, and taking a bus with the delegates to attend the Democratic convention in Atlantic City, NJ. This experience spurred me on to a dream of working in politics, so I applied to George Washington University (GW) in Washington, DC.

During my time at GW, I again was drawn to groups, joining Alpha Epsilon Phi sorority, later becoming vice president. Then, I became a volunteer at St. Elizabeth's Mental Hospital, serving in the geriatric ward and other wards. I learned along the way that when I helped other people, they would usually help me in return.

After graduating from college, I moved to New York City and got a position as an administrative assistant to the assistant director of advertising for a large corporation. I was shocked and disappointed, however, by the limited number of positions to which women in the company could aspire. During the 1970s, the business world was definitely a man's world. However, I decided to do my best to buck this trend and began attending NYU graduate school at night.

As I hovered between the two worlds of business and academia, my connections were limited to the few people I met at work and in school. Unlike high school and college, I had no time to join groups. I eventually got a position as assistant to the vice president of public relations and advertising at a big restaurant corporation. My boss took me under his wing, quickly showed me the ropes, and when he left the company for a higher position, I took on many of his responsibilities. When he was finally replaced, I asked for a promotion. I was promptly told that I should be happy to be the new guy's assistant and that was all I could expect.

That's when, at only 23 years old, I decided that I already knew everything I needed to know to start my own small business. Although I knew I still had a lot to learn, the connections I had made and samples of my work managed to land me several small restaurants as clients. Then, one day I got a small fashion client and delivered great results, which opened the door to more business. My fashion client's business tripled and they decided they needed a bigger PR agency. I was upset for about 24 hours, but then the female CEO who ran that big PR agency asked me to bring my clients over and work for her. I took advantage of the opportunity and learned how to run a bigger agency by establishing procedures, managing people, learning by doing every day. I didn't realize it at the time, but I was getting an on-the-job MBA. I worked my way up to vice president, and somewhere in the middle of all this, I managed to get married and have two children. I supervised big clients like Gap and Swatch watches, and my confidence and experience grew.

After 10 years at the agency, it was time for me to go out and start my own business again. My husband (and the unofficial president of my fan club) encouraged me to launch an integrated marketing/public relations agency that I decided to call Communications/Marketing Action (CMA). It was only one year after the 1987 stock market crash, and thanks to referrals, I attracted some good clients, like Revlon cosmetics and the Platinum Guild. I even hired a few employees; but then, after a few years, the business seemed stuck. I didn't know how to keep growing it, and I felt that I had no one I could to turn to for advice or support. I wasn't connected to other business owners, and I couldn't talk to my clients about internal issues. I knew I had to do something, so I hired a business coach. The best advice she gave me was to get out of the office and network with other business owners.

Not surprisingly, it worked. I had forgotten my connection habits from high school and college: how joining organizations, establishing myself as a leader, and supporting other people always led to good things for everyone involved. At my coach's suggestion, I joined the National Association of Women Business Owners (NAWBO). I decided to triple my efforts, so I also joined Fashion Group International (FGI) and the Ad Club of New York. I joined committees at all three organizations, connected with extraordinary people, and shared my expertise and connections. Over the next 12 years, I became chair of the special-events committee for the Ad Club, program chair and then secretary of the board of FGI, and finally, president of the NAWBO New York City chapter, and international chair for the national NAWBO organization. For the first time since college, I was linking out.

Since then, I have never been alone. I have been surrounded by major influencers, CEOs, and advisors to impressive companies, simply because I was willing to share my time. Both my past and present companies have benefited greatly from the relationships I made and maintained for 20 years, and I have continuously given my support and help to the people who helped me, as well as many other people I have met. Actively participating on boards, nonprofits, and the like are a critical part of the linking out strategy. As a bonus, I'm constantly surrounded by extraordinary leaders doing extraordinary things who also become friends and supporters for life.

I was able to build my personal reputation, my company's brand, triple my business, and launch new fulfilling enterprises that reflected my visions for success—all things I never could have done without linking out. This process impacted my entire life in positive ways that I could never have imagined at the time, and it will do the same for you, if you let it.

Link Out

It is difficult to share this strategy using only a few words. Something hit me one day, however, while I was listening to someone complain about spending long hours on social media yet still not connecting with anyone in a way that could help her career. It occurred to me that social media got it *partially* right. We do need to link to each other, and social media makes that possible. However, to truly build relationships, we need to link *out*; that is, we need to get out, go out, be out, and connect face-to-face with other people. We need to get up from in front of our computers, put down our smartphones, and meet up with people in the real world, not the virtual world. We need to talk over breakfast, lunch, coffee, or cocktails, in the restaurant, park, or gym, not just over e-mail and webinars.

Link out is a master plan for building long-lasting connections with people who will support your success. When you link out, you physically get out of your home,

9

office, business, career, and build face-to-face relationships. When you link out you will never have to feel alone again. You will always have people around you to give you advice, make introductions, and help propel you toward your goal. Sound good?

Link out is a process of getting out of your comfort zone, physically and mentally. It will help you build trusted collaborative relationships with people who are connected or linked to people who can make a difference in your life, and for whom you can do the same. Link out has no direct connection or affiliation to the phenomenally successful social networking site, LinkedIn. If you are a member of LinkedIn, however, it can be a helpful tool in linking out. (We'll discuss this in more detail in Chapter 6 of this book.) Linking out is a two-way street. You support people in becoming successful, and they do the same for you. Your initial reaction might be to wonder why anyone would want to support your success. It's all about the approach you take when establishing and building relationships. People want to help you when you help them. When you link out, your goal is to develop long lasting relationships that exist throughout your career.

This is neither about throwaway connections that are here one day, and gone the next, nor is it about use-'em and lose-'em relationships. That's the kind of old-school networking some people practice, and, as we discussed at the beginning of the Introduction, this simply doesn't work anymore. In the link out model it's not acceptable to meet people at an event, have quick conversations to size them up as a prospective customer, and exchange as many business cards as possible. By the time you leave, you can't remember one person that you met. Salespeople often look at everyone they meet at a networking event as a prospect. If the person is not interested in the product or service, it's bye-bye forever. That's no way to build a relationship.

In the link out model, you go to a networking event seeking out a few people with whom you have a strong connection or common ground. You then follow up after the event with the intention that the relationship will grow based on trust and mutual support.

Link out is a step-by-step process that can support you in achieving your wildest dreams. It is based on the premise that people will support you because they will succeed when you succeed, and vice versa. That is the way the world works. I'm sure you've heard the phrase, "what goes around comes around." My personal goal is to spread the link out master plan around the world so that, together, we ignite global economic growth and create a world with a thriving economy and fulfilled ambitions for future generations.

This book will teach you the benefits of linking out and creating your own entourage or support system. It will describe how it can change your life and help you realize your goals, dreams, and progress on your personal journey. Throughout the book, I will share the strategies that both past and present leaders have used to leave their mark and legacy.

These very same strategies work for those of us who have big goals or more modest goals and are content to live a happy life with simple desires. No matter what you have on your personal agenda, you will gain valuable insights on how you can achieve goals from the simple to the complex with an army of supportive warriors on your behalf. You will discover how to build solid relationships with people you never thought would be in your corner, determine where and how to find and engage your entourage of supporters, and what steps you must take to get there.

If you follow the advice of this book,

- Your network will share information and advice.
- You will be involved in associations on the leading edge of your industry.
- Your network will connect you with people that you need to know for whatever your situation.
- You will learn about the most important resources for staying ahead of the curve.
- You will have access to the knowledge, opinions, and mindset of leaders of a changing business, economy, and world.
- Social media will be at your fingertips for trends, articles, and connections.
- You will have people to support you in knowing what you need to know to continue your career in your current company or be prepared to move on to a new one.
- You will be ready to start a new business or consulting firm, or grow your current one, to meet the challenges of today.

If you are doing well in your career and want to ensure that this continues; if business development, marketing, and sales are a key part of your responsibility; and if you'd like a constant flow of customers with less pain and stress, then this approach is for you. This book can also be a life-saving tool for those struggling with business or career—people who are almost at their wits' ends or concerned about what next year or the next decade might be like. Once you put the link out strategy into gear, your concerns will lessen and confidence will reign, even in challenging times.

As you read this book, you will easily be able to apply its theories to your life via step-by-step processes, and track with an accountability form that I provide. I am committed to your success; but in order for link out to work for you, you need to be committed to your success, too. So let's get started figuring out how link out will make that happen.

Everyone Needs an Entourage

1

It is literally true that you can succeed best and quickest by helping others to succeed.

—Napoleon Hill, ***Think and Grow Rich***

Y ou may be wondering exactly what I meant when I told you in the book's introduction that you need an entourage. I'm not referring to the old-style entourage that surrounds royalty and A-list celebrities or the kind that follows the Queen to serve her every need: opening doors, fetching her lunch, having her hanky ready when she sniffles, and bowing and curtsying to acknowledge her wonderfulness. That traditional kind of entourage is useless; it merely serves as an appendage to superstar celebrities, who gallivant throughout the world with their make-up artists, hairdressers, nannies, assistant nannies, teachers, and parents-in-law all in tow. This entourage serves one person and gets nothing in return, except a paycheck or maybe, an occasional smile.

What you need is the new kind of entourage, the one that functions more like a team. Think of the Seinfeld gang, the Beatles in their heyday, or a World Series Championship team. This is a mutual fan club in which everyone is cheering

Table 1.1 Network versus Entourage

Network	Entourage
One- or two-time connection	Life-long relationship
A stack of business cards	People you talk to regularly
Forgets your name	Returns your calls and e-mails
One-way support	Mutual support—people help each other
Quick surface communication	In-depth, sincere communication
Inconsistent follow-up	Reliable follow-up
Call/e-mail only when they need something	Call/e-mail to make introductions and referrals
Self-win attitude	Win-win attitude
No interest in your personal life	Interested in your professional *and* personal life
Lack of trust in the relationship	Trusted relationship

one another on to victory and success. The new entourage helps its members achieve their goals, get the jobs and clients they want, move up the ranks in the corporate world, and start and build businesses, all by providing constant mutual support.

An entourage is different from a network insofar as it is built on trusted relationships among people who can count on one another to lend advice, support, and introductions on a long-term basis (see Table 1.1). A network is made up of people we meet, but not necessarily people we can rely on to help us. People in our network might help us if it suits their own goals; however, they are not necessarily consistently trustworthy for the long term.

The new entourage is like the solar system with the sun at the center and the planets rotating around it. Each planet is different, and brings its own unique qualities to the solar system.

The planets are the sun's entourage. They are always there; the sun can depend on them, and the planets depend on the sun as well to provide warmth and light. There's a mutually beneficial relationship between the sun and the planets, just as there is between you and your entourage.

In addition, each planet has its own moons revolving around it. Because they, too, are part of this solar system, this creates even more mutually supportive relationships. That's exactly how the new entourage works. Each of us is the sun in our own solar system.

The new entourage gives you great advice, ensures that you receive valuable introductions and referrals, and surrounds you with a group of influential people who offer their support throughout your career. In order to create these trusted relationships and establish a long-lasting entourage, your role is to do the same for them. Each member helps each other and then pays it forward.

You can also think of your entourage as your informal board of directors. There is a good reason that the members of most public companies' boards of directors are employed elsewhere: They don't have a direct stake in the company by working there. They take an outsider's view of the company's activities when they're appointed to guide, counsel, and advise a company's CEO.

If you think of yourself as the CEO of you—your career, your path, and your decisions—then it makes perfect sense for you to have a board of directors. You may not always know what's best for you, and it's probably difficult for you to take a step back and analyze your own situation, but your board can see things about you more objectively. You don't also know all the people that your board knows. As such, these advisors of yours can introduce you to people who can help you, as CEO, run you, your career, and your business much more effectively.

If it sounds to you as if there's some work involved here, you're right. There is. You may even wonder if it's worth the effort to link out. I can only say what millions of people have discovered since the beginning of time: life is better together.

If you like people, linking out will be easy and fun. Of course, it might be a bit more difficult if you're more introverted. If you are a loner, it might make you a little uncomfortable at first, and you may have to push yourself. You may be inclined to work at your desk all day, and then go home and plop in front of the TV and the computer instead of linking out. That's exactly what I felt like doing plenty of times myself—especially, after I had prepared dinner, cleaned up, and helped my kids with their homework. I'm sure many people have felt this way, but believe it or not, in the end it's not the easy way I once thought it was. I had to learn to stand up for myself and my own goals to get the help I needed from family, friends, neighbors, or babysitters so I could go out and link out.

If you have ambition, the so-called easy way out is a road that never ends. It's like a maze that constantly keeps you from finding the route to your next accomplishment. But once you start to link out, you find partners to help you on the road. They take you by the hand to show you the way to the golden door at the end of the maze. And the effort you make to find and connect with these people is worth it because *you* are worth it.

Who Do You Want in Your Entourage?

The ideal entourage is composed of influencers and people who are connected to other influencers and achievers. You want to surround yourself with self-sufficient, self-confident, and self-fulfilled individuals. You do not want people who are interested in themselves and their own success exclusively in your entourage.

Your entourage could consist of professionals from all walks of life: teachers, lawyers, accountants, artists, small business owners, executives, and more. Although you might assume that you should limit it to people from your industry or walk of life, a true entourage has members with a range of expertise from various fields. They are involved in businesses, corporations, communities, nonprofits, government, or other outside activities. They are doers. They may be movers and shakers. They are active, busy people who are making a difference in their own jobs, businesses, industries, and even in the world. These are the ideal candidates for your entourage. They may be friends, members of your family, or people you don't even know yet, but you will get to know them after you put the link out strategy into action.

For now, consider the notion that anyone that you like, find interesting or engaging, or anyone who shares a common interest or goal could be a candidate for your entourage. As you progress in building your entourage, you may discover that people in particular related industries can be the most valuable to have in your entourage. If that's true for you, then seek out more of them. However, consider that people with diverse experiences will help you in diverse ways.

It Takes an Entourage

The most successful people in the world have many things in common, and one of them is that they all have entourages.

It is widely acknowledged in the business world that success depends on the efforts of a team, not just one individual.

When famed inventor Thomas Edison was asked why he had a team of 21 assistants, he said, "If I could solve all the problems myself, I would." Management guru Ken Blanchard accurately pointed out, "None of us is as smart as all of us." Similarly, Stephen Covey, author of *The 7 Habits of Highly*

Effective People, said, "Interdependent people combine their own efforts with the efforts of others to achieve their greatest success."

Think about it. "None of us is as smart as all of us"; well, that's a no-brainer. As brilliant as someone may be, we are all limited by our own knowledge, experience, and the people with whom we have had relationships. When we have an entourage, we have access to people who think differently than we do. They look at challenges and opportunities in an entirely different way. They know people that we don't know.

So if all these leading business experts and authors espouse the value of teamwork to help us produce winning results, why do individuals go it alone in launching and growing their careers? Why do so many small business owners think they have to do it all by themselves? Why do many marketing and salespeople believe the only way to find new customers is by cold calling or snooping them out without a little help from their friends? Why do so many believe that if they can't succeed on their own it must mean they're failures?

These beliefs are false. We unfairly burden ourselves with an extremely heavy responsibility, and that load could be significantly lightened if we asked for and accepted the help of others.

Look at most of our greatest leaders; they did not do it alone. When members of the world male power circles refer to the "old boys' network," they are really talking about their entourage: a group in which they invest time and energy to build strong, trusted relationships. Many of those relationships began early in their careers, and they continue to add new connections to their entourage as they climbed the ladder of success.

A Look Back at History

Henry Ford is well regarded as one of America's greatest industrialists, yet he would never have achieved his towering success without his entourage. Napoleon Hill's book *Think and Grow Rich*—first published in 1937—tells Ford's story in detail. After working as an engineer for Thomas Edison at the Edison Illuminating Company early in his career, Ford started his own business and ultimately invented the first automobile after countless failures. Some of Ford's greatest achievements came as a result of the support of his entourage, which included his former employer Thomas Edison; Firestone Rubber Company founder Harvey Firestone; literary naturalist and Henry David Thoreau follower, John Burroughs; and agricultural scientist Luther Burbank.

Even President Warren G. Harding became part of Ford's entourage. The Ford/Edison entourage consistently supported each other's businesses and professional aspirations. They even participated in a series of camping trips together, traveling with what could be considered the first recreational vehicle (RV). Much of the back story of Ford's success involved the role that Thomas Edison played in encouraging this promising employee to continue to develop the self-propelled vehicle—later known as an automobile—while he was working at Edison's company. When Ford gained enough funding to leave and work on his project full time, Edison continued to support his success with advice and introductions to his entourage.

Gloria Steinem is famous for leading the women's rights movement of the late 1960s and 1970s and for founding several organizations that promoted gender equality. Steinem's success in gaining equal economic opportunities for women was a result of her leadership. However, change would have been impossible without the support of her entourage, which included attorney Flo Kennedy, US Congresswomen Bella Abzug and Shirley Chisolm, writer and feminist Betty Friedan, voting rights activist Fannie Lou Hamer, and civil rights activist and journalist Myrlie Evers, to name a few. It took a team effort to change the world for women.

Martin Luther King is the acknowledged leader of the Civil Rights Movement, but he couldn't have ended segregation without his entourage. It included civil rights luminaries like Whitney Young, Dorothy Height, Roy Wilkins, A. Philip Randolph, and John Lewis, all of whom were just as dedicated to achieving equality for African Americans as Reverend King was. All these individuals worked together, supporting one another's organizational goals to lead the way to civil rights for all, despite the fact that they each had his or her own, sometimes competitive, goals.

Back to the Future

It's amazing how powerful we can become when we are willing to reach out and ask others to help us, and it is equally amazing how powerful we are when we help others reach their goals. The historical examples cited throughout the chapter illustrate how we can each become agents for social change, groundbreaking innovation, or whatever our goals happen to be. History shows us how imperative it is to engage others in our cause, whether it is social, political, business, or even personal. The power of engaging an entourage makes *all* the difference.

The stories presented throughout the chapter can help us all learn from the past and move forward into the future by using what works in the present. I'm a big believer in crowd-sourcing wisdom from others. When I think about relationships, teamwork, and building your entourage, I'm drawn to what others who have "been there, done that" have said on the topic. That's why their experience is our insight to be followed for our future success.

Teamwork is so important that it is virtually impossible for you to reach the heights of your capabilities or make the money that you want without becoming very good at it.
—*Brian Tracy, management expert and author of*
Earn What You're Really Worth

Relationships are like muscles—the more you work them, the stronger they become.
—*Keith Ferrazzi, author of* Never Eat Alone

Lots of people want to ride with you in the limo, but what you want is someone who will take the bus with you when the limo breaks down.
—Oprah Winfrey

All these experts—people who have enjoyed such success in their own lives—cannot be wrong.

24

Link Out

They tell us, quite explicitly, that in order to achieve what you want in your life, you absolutely must surround yourself with people who are willing to help you realize your goals. They also tell us that we need to help our helpers as well, and be there when the going gets rough for them as much as they are for us.

The way these leaders created their entourage was to link out. They knew that the most important work they did was not getting done at their desk. Making personal connections in face-to-face situations was a vital part of their efforts. They got up from their desks, left their daily routine, and linked out to build new relationships. They joined associations, attended gatherings and conferences, scheduled breakfast or lunch meetings, volunteered their time to causes that mattered. Some entourages, like Henry Ford's, even went on trips together. Today, business and political leaders alike build their business and personal relationships at conferences like the World Economic Forum in Davos and the Allen & Company Sun Valley Conference, as well as at golf and spa retreats. These incredibly successful people all know one thing: concentrated face time forges strong relationships and builds entourages that last a lifetime.

The following chapters will teach you precisely what steps you need to take to successfully link out to build your system of friends, contacts, and colleagues into a supportive network of people—your entourage—who will help propel your success. Your responsibility is to do the same for them, because, as I've emphasized already, linking out works in two directions. People help one another to achieve their goals.

25

Everyone Needs an Entourage

Linking out is *not* a competition. It's a mystery to me why so many feel that building supportive relationships is akin to conspiring with the enemy, and such people see anyone who does something similar to what they do as competition. Wake up world! We can *all* be victorious when we work together. Yes, it may appear on the surface that we are competing. When we dig down, we discover that most of us have different goals and different definitions of success. By forming partnerships we realize that the person or business we initially perceived as competition can become a valued partner. This is true for individuals as well as companies. Several books espouse the belief that cooperating with companies that one may consider competition leads to positive results for both parties. James F. Moore's *The Death of Competition* is one such book; *Co-Opetition* by Adam Brandenburger and Barry Nalebuff is another. As President Franklin D. Roosevelt said,

Competition has been shown to be useful up to a certain point and no further, but cooperation, which is the thing we must strive for today, begins where competition leaves off.

In other words, the sooner you stop looking at your colleagues as competitors and start seeing them as collaborators and potential partners, the quicker you will be on your way to achieving your definition of success. When people take time to truly get to know one another nowadays, and explore how they can support one another's goals, then everyone wins!

The Power of a Link

Think of a silver, gold, or platinum chain around your own neck or that of someone you love. One link is connected to the next link, and each leads to another link. That's the power of linking out. When you establish a strong relationship with one person and you share your vision or goals, they have the opportunity to link you with another person and another person. Each link has its own chain of connections and relationships, and when you link out, these connections and possibilities can go in absolutely *any* direction.

Think how much more we glow and inspire others when the shine from those links surrounding us reflects on everything we do. It's almost magical. Sometimes my life does seem like magic—as though I found the pot of gold at the end of the rainbow. My life has been exciting and fulfilling because of linking out. I never would have accomplished all that I have without the magical power of the link. Now the power of the link can be yours, too.

2

The Foundation for Attracting Your Entourage

Vision without action is a daydream. Action without vision is a nightmare.

—Japanese proverb

Some people find it easy to make new friends, but, for most people, it is not that easy. Most of us have a small circle of a few really good friends—people who we trust and will share our feelings. Often, we have an even smaller circle of people with whom we feel comfortable discussing career or business issues. Your current network can help you achieve your goals by adding more trusted relationships.

The key to changing your career or business is growing your entourage and building on the relationships you have. Linking out is all about taking the skills and contacts you have to the next level. To attract people to be in your entourage, you need a toolbox of tactics. You already have these tactics available to you, but you may have not used them in a long time. They may be out of date or possibly it is time for a tune-up.

The tactics you need in your toolbox are your

- Vision statement
- Personal billboard
- Marketing plan

To assist you on your link out journey, I recommend you keep a journal dedicated to this journey. It will help keep you focused and organized, and it will play an important role in your success.

Vision Statement

Let's start with the most important tactic in your toolbox, your vision.

What is your vision for your career or business? It may be buried in your brain somewhere, but it's there. This book is going to help you discover it.

Visualization is more than positive thinking. It is an active process that helps you achieve your goals. According to Webster's Dictionary, a vision is

the act or power of anticipating that which will or may come to be. Or to put it another way, an experience in which a thing or event appears vividly or credibly to the mind, although not actually present.

Regardless of what stage of your career you are in, a vision can be equated to the experience of looking into a crystal ball and seeing your future life in action. It's useful to have a short-term vision of what your business, career, or life will look like in two years, and a longer-term vision of about 7 to 10 years from now. It's up to you how many years you would like to look ahead. Consider the fact that, 15 years ago, companies would usually consider a short-term plan to be five years, but today, they are more apt to have a two- to three-year plan. Things are changing so rapidly that, if we plan too far ahead, the world looks totally different than we had anticipated, so our strategies and our goals may change, too.

Why is having a vision important? It's as important to have a personal vision as it is for a corporation to have a business vision. When we have a vision, then we can create the strategies to make our vision a reality. If you don't have a vision, it's very much like traveling on a road with no destination. You might have a good time while you are traveling, but you have absolutely no idea where you are going to end up. You could be disappointed with your destination because you never planned to arrive there. When we have a vision, we can make a plan for our journey and make every effort to arrive at the destination we desire.

Personal Vision Quiz

To help you bring your vision into focus, start by taking a deep breath. Next, let your mind wander while you take this Personal Vision Quiz, writing the answers under the heading Personal Vision Ideas in your link out journal. Relax and give yourself at least 20 minutes to complete the quiz. It will provide you with the answers you need to shape your personal vision.

Part 1

Take some time and answer these questions:

- Why do you do what you do?

- What else, if anything, would you like to achieve?

- What satisfies you about your current work/profession?

- What do you feel most passionate about?

- If you could do anything, how would you like to spend eight hours each day?

- Describe the people with whom you would like to be collaborating.

- What results and returns are you presently getting for yourself?

- What are the results of your efforts for others?

- What excites you about what you do today?

- What excites you about your future?

- What do you see yourself doing five years from now?

Part 2

After you have answered the questions in Part 1, close your eyes, sit back, relax, and dream a moment or two. When you begin to get some images in your mind, you are visioning. Usually, if you allow yourself to be quiet for about 5 to 10 minutes, you will begin to see in your mind's eye what makes you happy or fulfilled. Do not exclude your personal pursuits.

When you feel strongly about your vision, you can make it happen, if you choose to do so. You may need to try this process a few times, giving it time to percolate. It is important to overcome limited thinking. By opening your mind and creating a vision statement, you're taking the first step to reach your goals.

You may immediately latch on to your vision. It may come to you in the shower—the place where many people get their best ideas—or as you awaken in the morning. Keep a pad and paper by your bed, so you can jot down your thoughts when they come to you. Give yourself the time and space to allow your vision to surface. It's a work in progress.

If your vision isn't clear, here are some steps to get you closer to it:

- Take time to look at your answers to the Personal Vision Quiz, Part 1.

- What similar answers do you have, and how do they link together?

- How do they relate to what you are doing presently or things you have considered doing?

- Integrate those answers with any pictures you see in your mind while you are taking Part 2 of the quiz.

- Write it all down.

- Leave it by your bedside table and take a look at it before you go to sleep and when you awaken. Within a few days, you will most likely have a vision, or the beginning of a vision for your future.

- When you do feel you have direction, write it down in a statement form as if it is already happening. Use positive words in your vision statement. For instance, say, "I am doing such and such." Avoid saying: "I am *not* doing such and such." When you write a negative, the mind picks up on it and focuses on it, instead of on the positive.

- Write your vision statement on a small card. Keep it by your bed or on your desk and look at it each night. If it makes you feel good and resonates with you, congratulations, you have your vision statement! It's fine if you continue to evolve it as your vision becomes clearer.

As an example, I created this vision statement one year before I created the concept for Women's Leadership Exchange: "I am helping women become more economically independent so that there will be more women leaders in the world."

At the time, I wrote the statement, I had not figured out the model for Women's Leadership Exchange, nor the name, or anything else. The concept came from me focusing on my vision. Suddenly, it all came together, and I knew how to make my vision a reality; Women's Leadership Exchange was born.

Vision Success Stories

Most successful people attribute their success to having a vision. At the time they create it, they often have no idea how to make it a reality, and yet ultimately, it does. How does this happen? When you focus on your vision, your subconscious mind leads you to direct your energy to achieve it.

Changing your thoughts can change your reality. A vision, when powerful enough, is accepted by our subconscious mind, and this leads to a change in mindset, as well as our habits and actions. This positive change brings us into contact with new people and situations. When you look at people who have succeeded in a given field, the trajectory of their success can be attributed to their clear vision and to the power of the subconscious mind. This has been documented by research going back to Freud, Napoleon Hill, and Dr. Joseph Murphy, as well as more research from leading universities like Yale and Princeton.

Martha Stewart

As a young wife, Martha Stewart loved entertaining, cooking, and working in her garden. While in her thirties, she had a vision of operating a popular catering company in her town in Connecticut. She became one of the most highly acclaimed caterers in the area. Once she achieved it, she expanded her vision. In her new vision, she saw herself as an author and television personality. Within a few years, she achieved that. Next, she created a new vision of publishing magazines, creating products, and building a powerful and influential brand. Needless to say, she transformed this vision into the Martha Stewart empire. Even a brush with controversy, and a brief jail term for a white-collar crime, did not stop her from keeping her eye on the ball. It is a good lesson for everyone. We all have challenges. When we continue to

35

persevere, visualize our goals, and refuse to buy into failure and self-pity, we can achieve our dreams.

Steven Spielberg

Three-time Oscar winner Steven Spielberg had a vision of being the best filmmaker of the century when he was only 12 years old. In order to earn a Boy Scout photography merit badge, he made a nine-minute 8-mm film called *The Last Gunfighter*. Not only did he earn that merit badge, but this sparked his vision. His biography describes Spielberg envisioning himself being presented an Oscar, and he began practicing his acceptance speech in front of a mirror. At 17, Spielberg got an internship at Universal Studios through an introduction by a family friend. Spielberg used this opportunity to approach famous actors like Cary Grant and top directors like William Wyler when he saw them on the movie lot. He approached them and persuaded them each to have lunch with him. By sharing his vision with them, he engaged them as mentors and connectors. They became part of his entourage.

Mark Zuckerberg

The youngest billionaire in the world, Mark Zuckerberg envisioned Facebook as a worldwide project that would change the way people communicate and stay in touch, and it ultimately became a billion-dollar company. Zuckerberg conceived of Facebook while attending Harvard. At that time, Facebook was viewed by his peers as a college project that might be worth a million dollars someday. No one took it as seriously as Zuckerberg until he cut short his college education to pour all his energy into developing Facebook. It was Zuckerberg's powerful vision that became reality.

Carly Fiorina

Carly Fiorina envisioned herself a leader in the field of technology. She began her career as a sales rep at AT&T in 1980, a time when there were few women executives in corporate America. She surprised her coworkers by joining the male-dominated Network Systems division and became that division's first female officer. Later, she became the head of North American sales. Her powerful vision, which most thought was unachievable, along with her outstanding sales instincts caught the attention of top brass at AT&T. Together they contributed to her success and led to her becoming president of Lucent Technologies and later Hewlett Packard. Most people were surprised at her promotions. Carly Fiorina's vision propelled her forward to become the most powerful woman in business in 1998.

In my research I discovered that most super-successful people all have visions of where they are going, and each person has an entourage. Sometimes, they formalize their visions by writing them down and posting them on their mirrors, refrigerators, or their computers. Sometimes, they do vision boards: collages made from magazine clips or artwork, which brings their visions to life. Some just keep their visions at the top of their minds at all times.

A colleague of mine was a publicist who was top-notch at her job. She worked for a small public relations agency, and later for a large public relations agency. She was loved and appreciated for her excellent results, especially for huge clients like airlines, toy companies, and other Fortune 100 companies. She grew tired of working for others and wanted to focus her energy on health, wellness, and spirituality, topics in which she was personally interested. She had a vision of working on her own representing some of the most respected experts in those three fields. She took a risk and left her job, and she kept her focus on her new vision. Within three months, she had connected with colleagues and editors, with whom she had developed relationships over the past several years. They became part of her entourage. Once she shared her vision of working with health, wellness, and spiritual experts, her entourage opened doors and connected her with experts they had interviewed, and publishers and agents who represented authors in those fields. Her vision and her entourage delivered. She quickly launched what would become a lucrative business working with the very people she had in her vision.

Most of the people whom we admire started with a vision of themselves devoting their energy to work in which they believe they will experience great satisfaction or achievement.

People who don't take the time to discern their vision often have jobs or occupations that leave them uninspired and unmotivated. We need to know where we want to go in order to get there. We need to know what we want to achieve in order for others (our entourage) to help us get there. Having a vision is critical to our success. Rarely is success accidental.

When you possess a vision, you can share it with people. The more you share it enthusiastically, the more people will want to support you in making that vision a reality. People are attracted to those who have a goal or a purpose in life. When you share your vision with passion, you will be surprised at how many people want to help you get there.

Your Personal Billboard

Once you have your vision in your mind's eye, write it down, work on how you phrase it, until it lights you up and makes you feel excited about your future. A warning to you perfectionists out there: Your vision statement does not have to be perfect. Just do your best to capture the essence of how you view your career, your business, your contributions, or your achievements. When you are able to express your vision statement with enthusiasm, it's time to take it public.

What's more public than a billboard on a highway? Thousands of cars pass highway billboards each day. They are big. They are bold. They get your attention. Some billboards try to convince you to buy a new product. Some urge you to make a stop along the way or change your destination.

Transform your vision into a personal billboard. A personal billboard serves the same purpose as a highway billboard, except it is promoting you, not a product or a destination. You can engage people with your personal billboard by sharing your vision statement, clearly, concisely and with enthusiasm.

For instance, Steven Spielberg's vision statement might have been "I am producing Oscar-winning films that inspire and bring joy to people of all ages." However, his personal billboard could have been, "Best film maker of the century."

What's on your personal billboard?

There are three steps to create your personal billboard:

Step 1—Answer the questions posed to you in the Vision section of this chapter.

Step 2—Build the dominant themes and ideas from your answers into a one- or two-sentence description of your vision for your future. Your vision statement is your personal philosophy that you can weave into conversations with potential members of your entourage.

Step 3—Take your vision statement and reduce it to a powerful phrase that can be displayed as your personal billboard informing the world who you are in the future.

You will use your personal billboard—the short version—to focus your attention on your goal. Create mini-billboards everywhere—on your computer, bathroom mirror, bed stand, and refrigerator—everywhere you look throughout the day and night. It will keep your focus on who you want to become by displaying it prominently. You will breathe it, feel it, and become it.

Once you begin to feel your personal billboard is real, you'll feel comfortable sharing your vision statement with more people, and you'll get closer to achieving your goals.

Marketing Plan

Use your vision to carve a marketing niche for yourself. With your vision and your personal billboard at hand, you are ready to market the *you* that you want to become.

It's time to put your marketing plan into action. Some people call this personal branding. I call it marketing *you*. People buy products when they are marketed and advertised effectively. You can use the same strategies to draw people to your personal brand. People will want to support you, because of your personal marketing campaign.

The rise of new technologies has increased the number of avenues available to market you. Establishing your personal brand is within reach through both in-person and online communications.

The four key strategies to successfully market *you* are:

1. Your entourage (Chapter 3).

2. Communications 2.0 (Chapter 4).

3. Entourage etiquette (Chapter 5).

4. Social media (Chapter 6).

Give-to-Get Philosophy

At the heart of your personal marketing campaign is a new attitude unique to most marketing programs. I call it the give-to-get philosophy. The give-to-get philosophy means you make the goals of your entourage more important than your own. The magic in marketing *you* successfully is based on building mutually supportive relationships. When you help people reach their goals, they are more willing to help you reach yours. Your generosity of spirit is present in all four marketing strategies. It is part of how you build your entourage, how you communicate, and how you use social media. When everyone has this generosity of spirit, it will be the hallmark of our society. Not only will all of us achieve our personal goals, but the world will be a better place for all of us.

The next few chapters will show you exactly how to put all four marketing strategies into action with the give-to-get philosophy.

LINK NOW: Five Tactics to Launch Your Link Out Program

1. Take the Personal Vision Quiz.

2. Create your vision statement

3. Adapt your vision statement into a sentence or two, which you feel comfortable sharing with people. Try it out, adapt it. Don't be deterred by what others may say. It's your vision statement, not theirs.

4. Write copy for your personal billboard.

5. Create mini-personal billboards on 3x5 cards and place them strategically where they will catch your eye throughout the day.

3

Recruit Your Entourage

Your real network is an overgrown jungle with an infinite variety of hidden nooks and crannies that are being neglected.

—Keith Ferrazzi, *Never Eat Alone*

I not only use all the brains I have, but all I can borrow.

—Woodrow Wilson, 28th President
of the United States

I t takes a village or a team or an entourage to get most worthwhile things done. It doesn't matter whether you are launching a company or launching yourself. It doesn't matter if you are leading a cause that can change the world or you are causing outcomes in your field of work. It doesn't matter if you are selling products and services or you are selling yourself. Going it alone will only get you so far. It will never get you—or anyone else for that matter—to your ultimate goal, to the top of the heap, to the peak of the mountain, or to the summit that you see in your mind. So why try to do it alone?

Your entourage will help you transform your vision into reality. In return, you will help them, too. When someone is in your entourage, you discover you are on the same wave-length. You feel connected and have a common bond. You believe in each other. Because you have formed a relation-ship based on trust, you listen to each other carefully, give serious consideration to each other's advice, and have faith in the people that you connect with each other. It's almost as if you've formed an extended family. In fact, often there is more trust between those who are in each other's entourage than there is among family members.

You may be asking, "Where in the world am I going to find people for my entourage?" This may sound like an impossible dream to some of you. I'm here to tell you that this is not as difficult as you may think. Most of you are going to enjoy engaging your entourage, especially if you are a people person. If you are not a people person, you might be ready to throw this book in the garbage and say "fuhgeddaboudit!" Please don't do that. I promise, I am going to make it as easy as possible for you. After you have followed the guidelines in this book and had a few successes, you will want to grow your entourage bigger and bigger.

First, let me tell you what I am *not* going to make you do.

- I am not going to tell you to go to networking meet-ings where the main purpose is to exchange business cards.

- I am not sending you to events where you must stand up and give your elevator pitch.

- I am not telling you to go out and give speeches in front of groups—the number-one fear of most Americans.

I hope you feel better now. Your worst fears are *not* going to come to pass.

On the other hand, if you want to do those three things, go ahead and do them. They can be effective ways to meet people. However, they are not the only way and they are not necessary to create your entourage. If you want to attend networking meetings, share your elevator pitch, and give speeches, do so with the purpose of building relationships with a few people you meet, people who could be part of your entourage. Don't spend your time giving out lots of business cards.

Entourage Qualifications

How do you know if someone is worthy of being in your entourage? How do you know if someone has entourage potential?

Marla Schaefer, former cochair and coCEO of Claire's accessories and jewelry with over 3,000 locations worldwide, says, "the best ideas that I've ever had in business have come from walking down a hallway and talking with somebody that was delivering the mail." She says most people believe that if people are not on your level, they have nothing to offer. She believes the contrary. "It's a great loss when people isolate themselves in their own world." According to Marla, "You have to be talking to everyone. . . . Keep an open mind, an open door and a ton of open-to-talk."

Open your mind to who could be in your entourage. They don't need to have an MBA, a PhD, or any other degree. They should be people who are active and enthusiastic about their professional work. Think about these six questions when you meet someone.

1. Are you impressed by the work they do?
2. Are they involved in an activity that sparks your interest?
3. Does their work have any commonality to your vision?
4. Do they have an interest or curiosity about your vision?
5. Are they active in associations or organizations that may give them access to leaders and decision makers?
6. Could they have clients, customers, associates, or connections with people who could be described by any of the preceding questions?

If you answered yes to at least two of these questions, those people are probably good candidates for your entourage. How do you find out this information?

- By asking them questions about themselves
- By showing them you are interested in them
- By getting to know them

Even if they don't end up as members of your entourage—you can still forge relationships that can benefit both of you. Most entourage members do not surface immediately. Every connection takes active attention until it develops into a first-class relationship that blossoms into membership in your entourage. So be patient, be generous, and be subtly present.

Now, it's time to identify *where* you will find your entourage.

Talk to Your Family

As I mentioned in Chapter 1, link out is a process of building trusted collaborative relationships with people who are connected or linked to people who could make a difference in your life. The fastest way to begin to build your entourage is to link out to people whom you already know.

Some of the members of your entourage are people already in your life. You just don't see them. In fact, they are hiding in plain sight. You may have even known them for years. They could actually be family members. The very same family members you have been enjoying Thanksgiving dinner with for decades. They could be aunts, uncles, or cousins whom you have known since you were two years old. Most likely you have never shared a conversation about your ambitions, your dreams, or your desires for your future. Have you ever asked them about their work, career, or how they spend their hours? Have you asked them what they care about or what they see in their future?

Most families don't have a clue what other family members do in their career. We're too busy talking about personal stuff, as well as eating, drinking, cooking, or watching sports on TV to even consider talking about professional matters. In the old days, the men used to retire to the drawing room to discuss business and current affairs and smoke cigars. Those conversations seem to have disappeared along with the drawing rooms. Sure, sometimes families discuss the news and politics, but rarely do they discuss careers and work. Most families just don't go there.

Since nobody goes there, nobody knows the hidden secrets about each other's careers. We may know Uncle Henry is an accountant or Aunt Jill is a copywriter. However, we have no idea what they actually do, who they work with, what they love about their work, and how they are making a difference in the world.

Can you imagine if we had authentic conversations with the ones we love about how we spend 40+ hours each week? What insights would we discover? What connections would exist? Do you know what Uncle Arthur does each day? You think he's in the publishing business, but that's about it. You know cousin Susie works at an Internet company, but you have no clue what she actually does there. Aunt Samantha runs an organization with more than 1,000 members. What was the name of it? You really can't remember. How would you know that Uncle Paul, the ad executive, works with Fortune 100 companies and knows all the chief marketing officers personally? Furthermore, he has no idea that you've been in the marketing arena for the last few years.

It would be fascinating to know what each of them actually does each day and to hear their goals or what they've accomplished in their careers. Back in the old days, people worked at the same company for a lifetime or they owned a family business. The world has changed. Today, people are changing jobs, launching entrepreneurial enterprises, doing all kinds of exciting things. Even if you knew what members of your family did five years ago, I'll bet their careers are quite different today.

In a rare conversation over dinner, a client of mine discovered that her niece wanted to be an interior designer. She introduced her to a business friend who owned a design firm to give her some information about the industry. Her friend was very impressed with the niece and offered her a job as an intern. Eight months later her niece moved up to a well-paid position as an assistant designer.

The key here is that a few family members could be supportive as you move forward toward your vision. You could be helpful to them, and they are not the only ones who can help you. They can connect you to the people they know. Each member of your entourage is a connector to other people who could be the golden nugget to your career or business success.

Start getting to know your family in a whole new way.

Invite your uncle out for coffee next week. Ask a cousin if you can drop by her office at the end of the day to talk and learn more about what she does. Your aunt could be heading up a fascinating association, in which you could learn something and she could introduce you to influential people. First she has to understand what direction you are headed and what you envision for yourself.

Meet with your family. Share your personal billboard and your vision. Then they might be able to introduce you to the right people. No wonder no one in your family has helped you. They don't know what you are up to and what your goals are!

When you sit down with your family members to talk about work, don't treat it like an interview. See it as an opportunity to look for new things you may have in common beyond the family relationship. A few key topics to discuss are:

- How did they get started in their career, and how did it develop into their present role?

- What do they like most about their work?

- What interesting people have they worked with as colleagues or clients?

- What things do they wish they had more time to do both on the job and off?

- Listen carefully to what they say, but don't be afraid to point out some commonalities you share with them.

- Find out if there is anything you can do for them, or if there are people you could introduce them to in order to help them be even more successful than they already are.

Conversations with your family can open the door to information, connections, recommendations, even potential clients and customers. Remember, don't sell your family, listen to them. When you are a good listener, all kinds of opportunities can surface because you have given the other person the chance to tell their story. By hearing another person's story, you'll see common threads that solidify your connection that will enable you to help each other, whatever your goals.

Enlist the Wisdom of Your Friends

Some of us have a few friends and some of us have many. It doesn't matter how many friends you have. They are usually a source of support and a few of them just might be entourage members. Again, it's not what they can do for you, but people they may know, who could be a valuable connection.

Some friends talk about their work. Often, it is to complain about their jobs or the coworkers who are driving them crazy. After all, who can you complain to, but your friends? How about shaking up that conversation a bit? Instead talk about your future, where you want to go, who you would like to meet that could give you advice or make introductions. Some of your friends may be connectors.

They know people. In addition, to the people in their workplace or former workplaces, they could have family or friends who could offer you guidance, introduce you to potential clients, refer others to your business, or give you suggestions on the best vendors or websites to use.

Give them the opportunity to connect you to influential people by sharing your innermost thoughts about your vision and personal brand. Then ask them who they know that might be able to give you advice.

Remember, in building your entourage, you never ask for help specifically; you always ask for advice. Asking for a job or a sale is the fastest way to turn off your entourage. How can they even think of recommending you or introducing you until they get to know you?

Once they understand who you are, the vision you have for your career or business, or the passion you have for the products or services you are selling, they might find a way to help. I've found that people are most willing to offer support or introductions when they come up with the idea themselves.

Again, always *ask for advice*. Of course, ask people first what their visions are for their future? Your friends could use your help as well. The more you give to others, the more it will come back to you. Trust me. This is the way the universe works. Give and you will receive.

Tap into Your Professional Network

There are pros on the golf course, and there are pros all around you. The pros that I am talking about are professors, advisors, colleagues, bosses—past and present.

The professionals you have access to are dependent on where you are in life. If you're a recent grad, then staying in touch with your professors is a smart strategy. If you're further into your career or running your own business, then staying in contact with former bosses, colleagues, and clients and customers is an imperative.

For students or recent grads, there are professors, deans, teaching assistants, or coaches, whom you know from college or grad school. If you are still in school, the time is now to initiate those relationships. Make an appointment to see your professor. Share your vision and your personal billboard. Make an impression on them and most will want to support you in your quest. Ask them about their own life experiences in the field. Some of them could have had careers before they joined academia. Ask them what else they recommend you do to further your vision. Find out whom they know who could also provide additional guidance and advice to you. Most of them will be flattered that you came to them. This is the kind of conversation that makes their teaching even more interesting.

Professors can be a great source for internships, connections, and advice. If you are in school, or graduated in the last year, use the opportunity to include the academic pros to assist you in building your entourage. Be sure to stay in touch with them after you've graduated. Always keep them posted on your progress and ask if there's anything you can do for them. They just might invite you back to speak at one of their classes.

Jane Applegate, president of the Applegate Group multimedia production company, author, and small business expert, says her career as a journalist began when her professor submitted her work to a national journalism contest and she won. This award led to her first job as a journalist. He was the very same professor who took the time to tell her, "If you would stop chatting and pay attention, I think you could be a great journalist."

For those of you who are already in your careers or between careers, you will find plenty of pros in the workplace. It's your boss, your former boss, your boss's boss, or a colleague with whom you successfully collaborated.

Ways to Link Out at Work

1. Connect with at least two people at work with whom you have a personal affinity by inviting them to have lunch or meet after work for coffee or a glass of wine. If there are others you respect, add to your outreach in the same way.

(continued)

(*continued*)

2. Keep your conversations positive. Many coworkers get together to complain or vent about their jobs or their company, but that is not a productive use of your time. Instead, talk about your vision, ask about their passion, and agree to support each other in realizing your visions.

3. Identify people in higher positions at work whom you admire, and reach out to them. Let them know that you would appreciate getting to know them better and learning from them, so that you can perform your job better. Most people will be flattered and will make the time to meet with you. Use the tactics shared in the book to engage this person in your entourage.

4. Identify some associations that you could join that can help you on your job, and support you in growing your entourage. For instance, if you are in human resources, there are several associations, such as the Society for Human Resource Management, to choose from. If you are in retail, join a retail trade organization in your specific retail category as well as your local chamber of commerce. If you are in sales or business development, join a local or national organization that will help you build your entourage for sales leads and referrals. Often your employer will pay for your dues or event fees, if you can convince them that your membership will enable you to be more effective at work.

It's smart to work late. That is a great time to show your face, and connect with the influencers who are still working at their desks or hanging out in after-work conversations. Introduce yourself. Tell them what you are doing, and what your vision is. Once you've made the intro, the next time you see them, you can ask for a meeting to get their advice.

Think about people that you've worked for over the years. What skills did they have that you learned from? Which of those people had great connections in the industry you are interested in? Which could give you a contact list that could make your head spin?

When you have already forged relationships at a company, the key is to stay in touch with them, even after you have left the company. Yes, this includes those colleagues who may have quit suddenly or were let go.

It's never too late to reconnect with former bosses as long as you left on good terms. Definitely stay in touch with colleagues you respect. I love hearing from my former employees. I want to know how they are doing, and I am happy to help them with advice and recommendations.

Most employers like to reconnect—unless you left them in the lurch. Even so, some people have short memories. It can't hurt to go back, if you know that you did a good job while you were in their employ. I used to meet my former boss, who owned a public relations firm, for lunch almost every year. Several years after my departure to start my own company, she actually asked me if I was interested in buying hers. She was looking to retire.

55

Recruit Your Entourage

Link Out to Your Entourage: On Planes, Trains, and Waiting on Line

When you look around you, there are interesting people everywhere: people who could be connectors; people who could be in your entourage.

One of my favorite places for meeting people is when I am traveling. Sometimes I really don't feel like talking to anyone. I just plop down in my seat on a plane or a train and focus on my work or read a good book. I'm really not anxious for any conversation or interruptions. Other times I am not even paying attention to the world around me, but I may comment on traveling conditions or an incident that just happened and before you know it, I'm having a conversation with the person next to me. When that happens, who knows where it may go? Sometimes it leads to exciting places. On two separate occasions it led to me discovering a young woman and a young man, both in their twenties, who became part of my entourage, and me in theirs.

I met Adrienne waiting on line for a bus to Washington, DC, very early in the morning in the pouring rain. The line we were on was very crowded and I was searching for my umbrella. She offered to share her umbrella with me. Both of us looked like wet rags, but that didn't stop us from discovering where we were going and why. The bus was crowded and we sat next to each other. We were both exhausted and soaked, which can provide a great opportunity for camaraderie. In fact, the more uncomfortable it is, the better for forging a relationship. She spent most of the ride sleeping, and me working, but when we got about 30 minutes from our destination, she woke up and we launched into a deep conversation, which led to our connection. It's two years later, and she has since moved from New York City to Los Angeles to San Francisco. After meeting in person in New York several times, we continue to e-mail and speak on the phone. When I met her she was in a terrible job situation, and for a while she wasn't sure what she was going to do. She asked for advice, which I happily shared. In Los Angeles she started the company we had been discussing. In San Francisco she started a second business, so now she has two. I've continued to give her advice on her businesses. She's helped me with my speaking to college graduates.

Buchi politely sat down next to me on a crowded train leaving Washington, DC. Although he wasn't on the train more than 25 minutes (he got off at BWI Airport in Maryland) our quick conversation established who we were, what we were doing. He had recently graduated from college, and had an exciting job at the US Congress, but he wanted to start his own business. We exchanged business cards and I told him to contact me. I heard from him a few weeks later, just saying hello via e-mail. Since then, he's recommended me for a speaking engagement and asked me to give advice to a friend, who was starting a website for women in business. I've given him pointers on a few things he's pursuing. He's a terrific young man, and I am happy to be there for him. He totally gets that it's not all about him. Being in one's entourage is not a one-way street, and, yes, young adults are in a position to recommend seasoned adults. Age or position doesn't matter.

So forget all those barriers that have stopped you from talking to people and go for it. The worst that can happen is that people you approach just won't want to talk. So you back off. If you approach people politely and respectfully, chances are they won't mind a little conversation, and you might start a great relationship, just like Adrienne and Buchi did with me.

Join Your Community

Joining professional, lifestyle, and charity groups opens doors to meeting new people who can be part of your entourage. A powerful connection is formed with people whom you share a common interest and purpose. You get to know them in a friendlier way, with no pressure to do business together. This can create a real relationship.

Before Hiroko Tatebe founded the Global Organization for Leadership and Diversity (GOLD), she was director, executive vice president, and treasurer of Dai-Ichi Kangyo Bank in Los Angeles. Prior to achieving that prestigious position, she was an assistant vice president with little insight about how to get promoted. There were few women at her level, and no women at higher levels in the bank at the time, so she couldn't even seek out a mentor. She hoped that by joining business associations, she might learn what she needed to know to grow her current role. By joining business associations like Financial Women International and Women in Business she met women executives from other corporations who were vice presidents, senior vice presidents, and CEOs of their own companies. Several became mentors to her, sharing their own experiences and offering advice. She credits those relationships, along with her growing expertise, to her rise at the bank. When she decided to launch GOLD, which is dedicated to building a bridge between Japan and the United States and helping Japanese businesswomen advance their status, it was her growing entourage that connected her to the people she needed to know to launch and grow the organization. Her activism in associations and the resulting relationships were the key to her achievements.

Start Your Link Out to the Community Effort

1. Engage a colleague or friend in the link out process. Not only will it be more fun, but you can also both push each other forward, keep each other motivated, and share resources, events, and so on. Arrange to check in once a week on how you are doing and share nuggets from the book to keep you linking out.

2. Select one day a week to attend association meetings, workshops, or networking events. The actual day of the week can change each week, but try to be in action for at least one day to propel yourself forward to make new connections. Once you get going, add a second day for linking out.

3. If you find it uncomfortable attending events by yourself, arrange to go with someone you know. Agree to go together, but once there, strike out on your own. Take a deep breath and introduce yourself to others;

(continued)

(*continued*)

use the communication tools in the book. If you meet someone who is well suited to your colleague, introduce them at the event; and your colleague should do the same for you.

4. Invest in becoming an official member of at least one association. If cash is short, give yourself a monthly budget to spend on attending worthwhile events, where you can meet potential entourage members. If you are able to invest more in linking out, then join two groups, or join one association and one nonprofit organization. If the group benefits from your effectiveness on the job, then your company may be willing to pay for you to join the association and/or attend the events.

The best things happened in my career when I started linking out to my community. Over the years, I've been a member and a board member of the Fashion Group International, the Jose Limon Dance Foundation Board, the SBA Advisory Council, NAWBO, and many more. I learned quickly that paying membership dues and attending events was only the first step in building relationships. I networked at the events, sharing brief conversations and the usual exchange of business cards. When I took the second step and volunteered to serve on a committee, the benefits were countless.

When you join a professional association or charity group, the first thing to remember is that the more involved you are, the more you benefit. The more you contribute, the more value you receive, the more your entourage will grow. Here's how to get started:

- Meet the chairs of the committees. Find out what they do, what their committee does, and how the organization measures its success.

- Let them know you are interested in joining a committee, but you want to join the one where your skills fit the best so that you can make a difference.

- Join and move into action fast, just like you would in a new job. Most associations operate more informally than companies. Most of the workers are volunteers who have regular jobs. Let people see you in action, getting results; they will be impressed.

- Take time after committee meetings to get to know the chair and other committee members. Meet for coffee, lunch, or a drink in friendly surroundings. Converse about similar topics that were suggested under Talk to Your Family, earlier in this chapter.

- Nurture the relationship when you connect with someone and you see them as someone you like and want to stay connected with. They just might be someone for your entourage.

In order to build relationships, people need to get to know you, see you in action, and hear your ideas. On a committee, people learn quickly who you are and how committed you are to achieve results by watching you and interacting with you. In my experience, this is the best way to grow your entourage. At the same time, you are learning by taking on new responsibilities, and you have access to senior-level people. You are getting to know people, and they are getting to know you, in a whole new way.

It's the in-person meetings that really count. Don't be shy about asking your fellow committee members to grab a bite or a cup of coffee after the meeting, to further discuss the projects that you are working on together. That's exactly where the opening happens. In the one-to-one, face-to-face situations, you can share your vision and learn all about others by asking questions and take relationships to a deeper level. This is how you will know if they will be part of your entourage. The relationships formed in associations can open doors for business development, advice, referrals, and jobs.

When I launched my integrated marketing firm in the late 1980s, the first association I joined was the Ad Club of New York. I signed up to be on the program committee because of my experience in special events. In addition, I had learned that this committee was in charge of the monthly programs, and selected industry speakers. It was a great way to show my effectiveness, support the ad profession, and connect with industry leaders. Though it wasn't my intent at the time, eventually, my active participation was instrumental in attracting several sizable accounts to my agency and building an impressive reputation.

As my agency began handling more fashion and beauty accounts, I joined Fashion Group International (FGI). Much to my surprise, at FGI, I made some of my best connections and friends. Several of the people I met on the program committee later became part of my entourage, and they still are.

I met Edie Weiner, one of the country's leading futurists, and Ann Stock, who at the time was vice president of marketing at Bloomingdale's. In the 20 years since I met Edie at Fashion Group, she has been a constant source of knowledge, insight, and advice, and best of all, of friendship. After I cofounded Women's Leadership Exchange in 2002, I was able to share Edie's brilliant insights on growing a business by having her keynote several conferences. Ann Stock went on to become the White House Social Secretary serving Hillary Clinton, and today she heads up Education and Cultural Affairs at the State Department. Ann's influence led to me getting involved with the Women's Leadership Forum, a political group for Democratic women leaders. My activism resulted in my being named chair of the New York State group. I took on the responsibility of organizing events for women candidates, raising funds and being a media representative. Perhaps one of my biggest honors was being able to introduce First Lady Hillary Clinton and Second Lady Tipper Gore to a room filled with supporters at Madison Square Garden. My connections flourished.

Simultaneously, I linked out to other community organizations by joining the National Association of Women Business Owners (NAWBO). Meeting other women who were more experienced than me in running businesses that were growing was huge for me. After serving on several committees, I became president of the New York chapter. My 10 years of being active in NAWBO included my traveling to national conferences around the country. Over the course of several years, my entourage grew to become national in scope. I built close relationships with women in Chicago, Atlanta,

Dallas, Los Angeles, and Phoenix. At the time, I didn't realize that this would later have a profound effect on my ability to launch Women's Leadership Exchange (WLE) nationally in its first year. My entourage was nationwide. Thanks to my entourage, cofounder Andrea March and I launched conferences attended by over 500 women in each of five major markets the first year. Women's Leadership Exchange could never have been launched so successfully without the advice and support of my entourage.

Never underestimate the results that we can each garner when we share our vision with our entourage.

Of course, this is not all about me. Nor is it all about you. It is about giving generously either directly or indirectly to our entourage. I gave my time, energy, and expertise to many associations, as well as to the people who were part of that community. People who believed in me rewarded me and returned the support by helping me achieve my vision. My vision became their vision, too. I could never have had the productive and fulfilling life I have had without my entourage. I continue to grow it as I pursue new ideas and continue to reinvent my career and renew my vision for the future.

When getting involved in your community, consider organizations that will enable you to learn, connect, and contribute. You want to participate in a group in which there is a need for your expertise or your energy, Look for organizations that are populated by members who are in your industry or a related one, or a nonprofit that serves a cause that matters to you. Meeting like-minded people can be a basis for building a relationship. To find these organizations, research the Internet or local media. The chamber of commerce, churches, synagogues, or your local government can provide you with contact information about all your community organizations.

An African proverb says, "It takes a village to raise a child." I propose we extend that proverb to "It takes a village to accomplish goals." This includes accomplishing your own goals, as well as the goals of the community. No one person can do it alone. Everyone is a winner when we connect with our community.

Create your entourage by linking out to your family, friends, professionals, and your community. Having an entourage makes everything possible.

LINK NOW: Five Tactics to Grow Your Entourage Faster

1. Become aware of how friendly you are at work, when you are traveling or when you are out in the world with or without your friends and family. Try starting conversations with people with whom you come in contact. Be willing to talk to anyone without judgment. Ask them about themselves first. Than share your vision and be open to new possibilities and connections.

2. Think about people you already know, including acquaintances or business colleagues, especially those who hold higher positions than you who you would like to know better. List their names in your journal. Invite them to join you for coffee or lunch.

(continued)

(continued)

3. Research and list organizations in your field or related fields, as well as nonprofits that interest you.

4. Find the local chapters of these organizations, along with contact information and a listing of upcoming events and meetings, and plan to attend several of them.

5. Organize a gathering of people that you like and admire for networking purposes at your home or favorite bar. Have all members of the group introduce themselves and share what's important to them or their vision of success. Use this as a jumping-off point for you to meet one-on-one with those you would like to consider for your entourage.

4

Communication 2.0

You can make more friends in two months by becoming interested in other people than you can in two years by trying to get other people interested in you.

—Dale Carnegie

W hat if I said, "You never have to go to a networking event ever again." Would you be happy?

Most people answer with a resounding yes and heave a sigh of relief. The people who tell me, "No, I wouldn't be happy. I like going to networking events," are definitely in the minority.

Most people go to a networking event with their mouths turned downward. Once they enter the room the smile goes on like a switch has been flipped. We are in acting mode. You can almost convince yourself you want to be there. We all go because we think it's the only place to make connections.

By now you have learned that there are many places you can go to meet your entourage, in addition to traditional networking events. Although networking events are not high on my priority list for building an entourage, if you like attending them, they can be worthwhile when you use the right link out strategy.

I am one of those people who learned to like networking events. (I used to hate them.) How did I learn to enjoy them? For one thing, I attend more events hosted by the associations and organizations with which I am affiliated, and I attend fewer independent networking events. When I go into an association networking event, I feel more comfortable, because I know several people there because of my personal involvement. When I do attend a nonaffiliated networking event, I use the link out strategy. I attend with minimal expectations and I behave differently.

This chapter will tell you how to use the time you spend at networking events most effectively. You will not be doing old-style business-card-exchange networking. You will meet people with the purpose of starting relationships who will help you grow your entourage.

The link out, no-networking strategy works for those of you who hate to network as well as those of you who like it. If you don't like to network, you can do a lot less of it. If you do like to network, you will adapt easily to the new link out style. When you are building relationships, you are building your entourage. It's no longer a race to gather as many business cards as possible. Instead, your goal is to meet two to three people you would like to get to know better.

It's Not about You

What do you think is successful networking? Are you the supersonic networker, the nebbish networker, or the self-absorbed networker?

Supersonic networkers go into a room with the goal of selling and meeting 10–20 prospective clients. They corner people whom they identify as targets, and they tell those people how super their own businesses are. They believe they are the center of the universe and think everybody should be interested in what they have to say. If the people they approach aren't interested, supersonic networkers leave with supersonic speed, showing absolutely no interest in their targets.

Then there are the nebbish networkers who wish they were not there, waiting timidly for people to approach them. Sometimes they force themselves to go up to people and start blah-blah-blahing about nothing, while not looking anyone in the eye. They are also totally focused on themselves and distribute business cards to anyone who has two legs. America's favorite nebbish, Woody Allen, did get one thing right when he said, "80 percent of success is showing up." If you stay in your office or continually check your smartphone, you are not showing up. Thanks, Woody, for the good advice, but when you do show up, don't make others wish you didn't by acting like a nebbish.

Finally, there is the self-absorbed networking type. This type has the tendency to go on and on about themselves and never asks you what you do, how you feel, or what you think? When you finally get the opportunity to get into the conversation, you notice their eyes darting around the room, looking for someone else to talk to, or they interrupt you to get in another few comments before you have even expressed a complete thought. Most networking events have their share of self-absorbed networkers, which is often why people hate to network. This kind of nonconversation is embarrassing, uncomfortable, and definitely a waste of time.

If any of these networking personalities describe you, then pay extra special attention to this chapter. You may recognize some of these snafus as your own. If that's the case, it's time to listen up!

In the world of building connections, it's not about you at all. It doesn't matter if you meet people at a networking event, an association or board meeting, or someone in your entourage has introduced you. You need to make the other person the star of the show. Your job is to make the other person feel important. That other person is the king or the queen of the conversation, and you are there to serve them.

If you really think about it, doesn't everyone want to feel important? We are flattered when someone treats us royally. Don't you love it when someone welcomes you and asks you lots of questions about yourself? Don't you love it when people give you their full attention, listening to every word you say? When people are attentive to what you say, aren't you predisposed to like them and want to get to know them better? Of course you are.

"When you make the conversation all about you, others may think you are clever," says Andrew Sobel, author of *Power Questions*. "But you will not build their trust. You will not learn about them. You will squander the opportunity to build the foundation for a rich, long-term relationship," he adds.

How Many People Do You Need to Meet?

The answer might surprise you.

Many people measure the success of a networking event by the number of business cards they exchange, meaning the more the better. To be quite frank, the only person who benefits from all these cards being exchanged is the paper manufacturer and the printer.

The real success when you network is discovering a few people with whom you truly make a connection. That could be one, two, or three people. What good is it to meet lots of people, if you don't have time to follow-up with them? What really determines success is the number of postnetworking meetings you schedule and how you connect at the second meeting. It is a great success if both of you find ways you can help each other in business, career, or even in your personal life. For instance, you might meet someone who can be in your carpool that lives in your neighborhood. You might find someone who loves to run and is looking for a running partner. Perhaps you can combine the personal with a business objective.

Susan Penfield, senior vice president at Booz Allen Hamilton, tells the story of how she snagged a huge contract with a government agency by making a strong personal connection with the decision maker. As part of the getting-to-know-you process with the government agency decision maker, Susan shared information about Booz Allen's volunteer program on behalf of The Children's Inn, a residential "place like home" for sick children and their families. Susan totally engaged the decision maker when she told her about the team-building that occurred when Booz Allen corporate teams contribute to the lives of at-risk children and their families, by cooking dinners and providing support at The Children's Inn. It turned out that the decision maker saw this as a great opportunity for morale building for her very own team at the government agency and was eager to put it into action. She was both impressed by Booz Allen's and Susan's commitment to The Children's Inn. For Susan, this resulted in both a strong personal and business connection. As a result Booz Allen got the government agency as a client, and Susan began a longstanding business and personal relationship with the decision maker.

Success is creating a human connection in some area of your life, which makes both people want to stay in touch. As you continue to get to know each other, you may find that you can be supportive to each other in multiple ways and that this person will come to be an important member of your entourage.

Rules of Engagement

To engage people in your entourage, there are certain rules that make it work. Although these rules apply primarily when you sit down face-to-face with a prospective entourage member, they also apply when you meet someone at an event or talk to them on the phone. These nine rules will help you build relationships that lead to a growing entourage of people who will support you in reaching your goals while you support theirs.

1. **First meeting**. First, introduce yourself briefly with a slightly expanded version of your personal billboard (Chapter 2). Second, immediately say that you are interested in hearing about them. For instance, "Enough about me. I'm really interested in hearing about you."

2. **Listen with your eyes**. Some believe that speaking well is the most important communication skill. I disagree. I believe that listening is even more important. Give your potential entourage member 100 percent of your attention. Look them in the eyes and take in every word. If you are like most people, listening does not come to you naturally. You may have to practice listening to your Mom, wife, husband, or your brother. In a real life situation, especially if you are having an engaging conversation, you may find yourself on the edge of your seat, waiting impatiently to jump into the conversation. Stop yourself. Don't interrupt them. Stop thinking about what you are going to say to them next. When you are thinking about your next comment, you miss what the person is saying. When you listen with your eyes and focus on what they are saying, you hear everything they say. Then you can respond more intelligently, more empathetically, and truly connect with the person on a deeper level. When you have heard them loud and clear, then the words coming out of your mouth will enable you to truly relate to them. That's what building a relationship is all about.

3. **The $64,000 Question**. Get the conversation and the relationship rolling by asking thoughtful questions. You can do this without turning your meeting into a 1950s quiz show. Asking questions can connect you personally giving your relationship a decided edge. Of course, it's easier to talk about yourself, but it is infinitely less effective in building a relationship. Asking questions proves you have real interest in the other person, and who wouldn't be flattered by that? Before you get to the meeting, plan the questions you want to ask, and be sure they are open-ended questions, so your companion will have plenty to say. A good question recommended by Andrew Sobel in *Power Questions* is, "Why do you do what you do?" A second one might be, "As you think about the future of your business, what are you most excited about?" Both questions get to the root of why someone is passionate about what they do. Chances are, after listening to their answers, you'll have some insightful comments, and now the conversation is off and running.

4. **Share your vision**. When it's your turn to speak, share your vision and what makes you or your business unique. It's okay to share your achievements and challenges, as appropriate to the conversation. Don't come off like a braggart, but don't demean yourself either. Be proud of what you have done and share it.

A sit-down meeting is an opportunity to share your challenges, ask for advice, and inquire about which people they may know who might help you. Because you gave them your complete attention, most likely they will do the same to you. Remember, do not go on too long. You are meeting with a busy and important person. Make sure you know how much time the person has to meet with you so they are not uncomfortable about breaking it off. Respect their time and they will respect yours.

5. **Ask for advice**. If you are pitching business or looking for a job, never say that's why you want the meeting. Your best chance of getting a meeting is by saying you value the person's advice. Sure you want a job or a new client or customer, but your best chance of getting one is to engage this person in your entourage. Not only will you get valuable information, but, also, if you follow the rules of engagement, you will get introductions to potential connections who could help you reach your goal. Your entourage is a source of a lifetime of connections and support. Remember, this person is one planet in your solar system. Hundreds of moons revolve around them. Any one of those moons could know of a job for you, but you must start by building a strong relationship with your entourage. Then they will connect you with a hearty recommendation.

How to Follow Up on an Introduction

1. First, ask your entourage member to answer the following questions about the person with whom they are connecting you, before you follow up:

   - What's your relationship with them?

   - What are your ideas of how we may be able to help each other?

   - Would you mind making an e-mail introduction?

2. Research the person being introduced on the Internet. Do a Google search, and check LinkedIn, Facebook, and Twitter. Before you meet or speak on the phone, look for commonality that you can reference in the conversation.

3. Once you have been introduced, immediately follow up with a friendly e-mail and request to meet or speak on the phone. Suggest a range of weeks, days, or times to connect.

4. If you know the person is very busy, always give them the opportunity to have a telephone appointment. Once you've had that call, and there is more for you to discuss, you can then suggest meeting in person. Be willing to go to them to make it convenient.

5. Always acknowledge your entourage member in the follow-up e-mail, by stating how much you respect them and how you've found their recommendations to always be worthwhile for both people.

6. After the call or meeting is scheduled, send a thank-you e-mail to the introducer.

7. Keep your entourage advised on the progress and results of the introduction.

6. **Create a collaborative relationship**. Once you have both shared, it's time for you to offer your support. Just because you may view the other person as on a pedestal, that doesn't mean you can't help him or her. Think of yourself as a connector. Who could you introduce that person to that would benefit that person's business. If you ask enough questions and listen carefully, you will have a sense of how you can assist or support the other person or make an introduction that would be valuable. If you don't, then just say, "How can I help you?" or "Who would you like to meet?" I conclude almost every business conversation I have with one of those questions. It means a lot to people. The offer alone goes miles in building a collaborative relationship.

7. **Be authentic**. Who are you and what makes you unique? Bring that to your connections. Do you like to tell jokes? Then tell them (though you might want to keep away from sexual innuendos and the like). Share your leisure-time activities. You may discover your connection enjoys the same diversions.

77

Communication 2.0

Encourage your connection to be authentic, too. Ask them questions about what they do when they are not working. You may discover you have things in common with them and now you can share them. If you admire the shoes or handbag of your new connection, then say so. Many women in business bond over fashion. The only off-limit category is politics. Tread lightly here. Don't assume you know your connection's political views. This can be a dangerous area until you know each other better and the relationship is well established.

8. **Stay connected**. Our contact lists are filled with names of people we used to be in touch with regularly. What happened to them? Did they move to Siberia? Did you? Probably not. You just lost touch with them. How do you stay in touch with all the great people you meet? After all, you do have to work. Here are a few easy ideas:

   a. Write a blog; send a link to the people on your list.

   b. Connect them to someone who could benefit their businesses or their personal lives.

   c. E-mail them an article that you think they'll find interesting.

   d. Invite them for coffee or suggest a quick 15-minute phone call to catch up.

   e. Keep a list of people you admire from your past and present. Create a plan to reach out to a certain number of them each week. Use a spreadsheet to track your success. You'd be surprised how happy they will be to hear from you. If they are not, then they aren't entourage material.

A good friend asked me if I knew anyone who worked with family-owned businesses. He was interested in expanding his market to offer his services to them. I went back in my memory and remembered an accountant with a firm that targeted that very market. I had lost touch with him and hadn't spoken to him in ten years. I researched him on the Internet and found out that he had sold his business and had relocated to a neighboring town. I had had a really good relationship with him and his wife, who was a NAWBO member, but somehow our paths went in different directions and we lost touch. I found them on the Internet and reached out. He was very happy to hear from me, so we arranged to meet for dinner and reconnect. In updating each other on our families and our new pursuits, we discovered we could again help each other. In addition, I connected my friend, who got great advice about family businesses. We are now in each other's entourage again.

9. **Be a long-term thinker**. As you meet people who could be in your entourage, keep in mind that building an entourage doesn't happen overnight. If it was as easy as sending a bouquet of flowers, then everyone would be doing it. By the way, sending flowers to someone in your entourage who helps you out is

a good idea!! Smart, successful people know that it is their entourage who made it possible for them to know the right people at the right time. That's why they never stop adding people to their entourage. A year from now, you'll look back and remember you had only a few people in your entourage, and now you have 12 or maybe even 20, and your life has changed for the better because of them. Can you imagine what next year holds? Keep it up. The future is yours.

When you follow the rules of engagement, you will not only grow your entourage, you will also be building your personal brand and improving your leadership skills. In fact, these are the rules that most successful and popular leaders follow to engage people in their causes, their companies, and their visions.

I am reminded of meeting former President Bill Clinton for the first time on a rope line at the White House. I will always remember how engaging he was and how good he made me feel about myself. Of course, he didn't have to introduce himself to me. I introduced myself very quickly and asked him a question (rule 1). He looked me directly in the eyes, answered me, and then posed a question right back to me (rules 2 and 3), making me feel my opinion was important to him. He seemed so interested in what I was saying by listening with his eyes that I will never forget that moment. He never looked away or rushed me. He listened intently, like I was the only person in the world at that moment, though the room was filled with people waiting to meet him (rule 2). Had I not been on a rope line with 150 people behind me, I'm certain the President would have followed the rest of the rules of engagement, and I would have done my best to follow them as well. President Clinton is known for his charismatic leadership and being an excellent communicator. We all have that potential. Want to be the best communicator you can be? Allow your inner charisma to come out by making the rules of engagement your own.

LINK NOW: Five Tactics to Make People Want to Know You Better

1. Prepare a few questions you want to ask them before the meeting.

2. Always ask about them, before you start talking about yourself.

3. Listen carefully to every word they say. It's fine to jot down a few notes to help remember what they say. In fact, I recommend it.

4. If they share that they have a need for something, think about how you or someone you know might be helpful. Offer to make an introduction. If a useful introduction occurs to you after the meeting is over, mention it in the follow-up note or e-mail you send.

5. Share authentically about yourself, and be sure to include your vision in the conversation. If you are just getting to know them, hold off asking for help for yourself until a second meeting. If they offer to help you without your asking, accept it.

5

Entourage Etiquette

Really big people are, above everything else, courteous, considerate, and generous—not just to some people in some circumstances—but to everyone all the time.

—Thomas J. Watson, Founder of IBM

When I was a little girl, my mother and my grandmother taught me manners. They said, "Leslie, manners are the niceties of life. If you don't have good manners, people won't like you." That worried me a lot because I wanted to be liked. So I tried really hard to learn proper manners.

My favorite poem about manners was "The Goops." I recited this poem to my brother and sister and later to my children hundreds of times.

Here's what I remember:

The Goops they lick their fingers.
The Goops they lick their knives.
They spill their broth on the tablecloth.
Oooooh, they lead disgusting lives.
The Goops they talk while eating

And loud and fast they chew.
And that is why that I am glad that I am not a Goop
Are you?

—Gillette Burgess

Despite the impact this poem had on me as a child, and perhaps on millions of other children, it seems to me there are a lot of Goops out in the world, and the number keeps growing. I'm not only talking about people with poor table manners. I am talking about people who disrespect each other and don't practice basic common courtesy. We used to call it being polite. Today it's called civility.

In the world of business and professional services, it's what I call entourage etiquette. If you want people to do business with you, hire you, recommend you, say glowing things about you, and be in your entourage, become aware of today's rules of civility to avoid being a twenty-first century Goop.

We live in a fast-paced world. E-mail, texting, and voice-mail have influenced us to use shortcuts to communicate. However, when speed causes us to disregard the general rules of etiquette from our communications, we may make a poor impression. Be aware of the impact of your words or lack of words in your connections with others.

In this chapter I will be sharing nine tips that may seem basic to you. If you have already been Goopified and are gracious and polite in all your dealings with people, then give this chapter a skim. If you think there's a chance your etiquette could use a bit of polishing, then consider that some of the rules shared in this chapter could be helpful in getting you in the door or in the conversation. Many financial services firms include an etiquette workshop in their training of new recruits. This suggests that almost everyone could benefit from a refresher course in etiquette in the world of business, particularly for those who are looking to build longstanding relationships.

1. **You had me at hello**. When you meet someone, shake their hand *firmly,* look into their eyes, smile, and tell them "it's great to meet you." It's the first impression—the gift that keeps on giving. Every time you meet someone and leave someone, you have a chance to make a first impression. Between the meeting and leaving, show them how happy you are to be there talking to them. Of course, always listen with your eyes, as described in Chapter 4 under "Rules of Engagement."

   When I had my marketing firm, before my team went out to pitch an account, I would say to them, "We're going to a party. We're going to meet new people and have a lot of fun." It worked. It put everyone in a happy frame of mind. It took the stress out of the meeting and our potential clients met a group of happy people that appeared to love their work. People are naturally attracted to positive energy. You might try infusing yourself with enthusiasm before you go to meet a new person. You might feel nervous, but as the slogan says, "Never let them see you sweat." People want to connect with people they like. They want to help people they like. They want to work with people they like, and, for the most part, that is happy, enthusiastic people.

2. **Follow-up etiquette**. After the meeting, when you get back to your computer or smartphone, be sure to send them a quick thank-you e-mail. Don't wait more than 24 hours to do this. Also, immediately write down a reminder to do anything you said you would do for them or any introduction you offered to make, so you don't forget. I do my best to follow through within 48 hours so my entourage knows I am trustworthy. I'll have more to say on trust and accountability in Chapter 9.

3. **Lock-down your cell phone**. While you are in a meeting with or without a meal or coffee, turn off your cell phone. The person with whom you are meeting is the most important person in the world while you are together. Make sure they feel that way. If you absolutely must leave your phone on, due to a potential time-sensitive matter, then put it on vibrate . . . and don't dare answer it unless you suspect the person calling is in serious trouble. When you are building a relationship, the only thing worse than being interrupted by a ringing cell phone, is answering it and talking to the caller. That can put the kibosh on a good meeting in five seconds. If you do this, it's inexcusable. If your companion does it, forgive them. Remember, you are the person building the entourage, not them.

4. **Three strikes and you are out**. When you send an e-mail and you don't hear back within five days, send it a second time. This time put the person's name in the subject line, along with "in case you missed my e-mail." Usually, this will get their attention and they will respond. If they don't, send the e-mail a third time with the same subject line.

Most people interpret the nonresponse as "I'm not interested." That's not usually true. Ninety percent of the time it means that they didn't get or didn't read the e-mail due to the following circumstances: the e-mail went into spam, the person is traveling, their mailbox is full, or your e-mail got mixed in with their junk mail. Seven percent of the time, they just didn't have time to answer, and then they got busy and forgot about it. You are not yet on their priority list. So don't take it personally. Three percent of the time, they aren't interested. Since 97 percent of the time, e-mail recipients want to stay connected with you, use the three-strikes rule. Keep trying to reach them until you strike out. By the way, always copy the person who referred or connected you to the person you are addressing. Then they will know you have followed through on what they recommended. If you don't get an answer after three tries, they can reach out on your behalf.

5. **Say thank-you three times**. There is nothing more important than saying thank-you to your entourage for (1) meeting you in person or talking on

the phone, (2) giving you advice, and (3) connecting and introducing you to someone who can help you. You can quickly lose your entourage when you take them for granted and don't show appreciation. There are a couple of options to pass along your appreciation. An e-mail thank-you is acceptable. I strongly suggest you send it immediately. Even better is a handwritten note. In fact, if there's any chance that your e-mail may have gone into spam, then definitely use the post office and send a handwritten note.

6. **Keep your entourage in the loop**. If an introduction was made, let them know immediately when you have scheduled a meeting. Follow up afterward to inform them of the result of the conversation. If your connection offers you advice, be sure to tell him or her how it went. When you get a job, a new client, a speaking engagement, or such, let them know about it and thank them, even if it came from a connector. Use every opportunity to stay in touch with them, to let them know how you are doing.

Here's a true story . . . my roommate from college sent me the resumé of her niece, Jennifer, who was fresh out of law school, and asked me to help her find a job. Of course, I said yes. I sent her resumé to my lawyer and asked if he would give her some advice in finding a job. Six weeks later, my lawyer called and told me that he had hired her. I was happy, but surprised. Jennifer had not called me to tell me that she got the job. I never heard from her. No thank-you e-mail, no update, no anything. I could have been in her entourage and been there to support her throughout her career. She got a job with my help. Without her thank-you or update, I felt disconnected from her and the situation.

7. **Prove you can be trusted**. Do what you say you are going to do, and do it within a week. If you don't or can't, then let them know you can't and why. If you want the support of others, you need to show them that you can be trusted. Trust is the number one value people look for when deciding whether to hire or recommend someone to a client. Trust is the great equalizer. When all things are equal in talent and expertise, trust becomes the number one factor. There are lots of experts and hard workers, but trust is a rare commodity.

8. **Treat others how you would like to be treated**. This has been known as the Golden Rule for centuries. Although it may sound a bit corny, it should be obvious to us. Yet in our haste to get as much done as possible in our day, we sometimes overlook doing the things we would like others to do to us. Ending your day by asking yourself if you followed this maxim could save you from losing some relationships and gaining some new ones.

9. **Pay it forward**. The more you give, the more you get. This is the unwritten law of the universe. Be

generous. As you build your entourage, continuously look for ways to help others. It comes back to you. It really does. You are the sun in your own solar system; keep it going and growing by helping all the planets and moons that surround you. Be an active participant in other people's solar systems. Be a planet—a source of advice and referrals to others. What goes around comes around.

In most countries around the world, etiquette is an unspoken law. Without it, no business is done. In Japan, it is standard operating procedure that a meeting starts and finishes according to schedule, unlike America where meetings often start late and end even later. The Japanese are known for taking copious notes, and there's a good reason. They will hold you to what you say and they have the evidence to back it up. I'm always surprised when people I am meeting with tell me they are going to do something by a certain date and they don't write it down. Do they have photographic memories?

In China, business people usually start with wining and dining, followed by a period of general observations and questions. The Chinese like to take their time getting to know you, and getting a feel of who you really are. A deal is never done at a first meeting.

The Spanish usually want to go to dinner or attend another social engagement with you before they will even agree to a meeting. In fact, the best way to do business in Spain is through an introduction of a mutual acquaintance to establish your character and credibility, just like the link out method.

Around the world, most top executives won't do business with another until trust is built. In the United States some believe they can do business and get business with the sheer force of their personalities and their salesmanship. More and more today, the way you treat people is the great differentiator. One might get the client or the job because of one's forceful nature, but how do you keep that relationship going? The tactics outlined here are consistent with how most of the rest of the world does business. If you practice linking out, then you will have the basic etiquette of doing business anywhere in the world.

A study conducted by Dan Kennedy, marketing guru, showed that 68 percent of clients who leave do so because they feel unappreciated, unimportant, or taken for granted. Generally, that is how most relationships end, too. Following the rules in this chapter enables you to show your entourage and the people with whom they connect you that they are appreciated. That is how you keep them loyal to you for a lifetime. Relationships should never be taken for granted. They are the magic potion for success in business and a satisfying life. So stay in touch with them, think of them often, and find out how you can help them.

> Politeness and consideration for others is like investing pennies and getting dollars back.
>
> —Thomas Sowell

LINK NOW: Five Tactics to Get Off to a Good Start

1. Practice entourage etiquette with your wife or husband, your parents, or other family and friends to break old bad habits, like checking your smartphone while you are having a conversation with someone, not giving them your complete attention when they are talking, and not looking directly in their eyes.

2. If you don't already own them, go out and buy some nice thank-you notes with the first letter of your last name engraved on them, so you are ready to say thank-you to your entourage the old-fashioned way.

3. Think about a recent instance in which you said you were going to do something for someone and you didn't do it. Or think of someone who did something helpful or nice for you and you didn't send a thank-you or e-mail a thank-you. Now just do it, even if it's a month late. After you did it, how did you feel?

4. Is something new going on in your life that you want to share with people with whom you would like to stay connected? Send out an e-mail to them, share your news, and tell them you would like to schedule a call or get together to find out what is new with them.

5. When you wake up in the morning, list three things you will do today to link out and add value to your entourage. Consider doing that every day.

6

Linking Out with Social Media

The telephone seemed magical at the time of its invention by Alexander Bell in 1876.

At long last, people didn't have to cross the street to talk to their neighbors. They could just ring them up on the phone.

E-mail was developed as an inner-office communications tool when it was conceived in 1982. Office workers didn't have to get up from their desks to ask a colleague a question. They could just send them an e-mail. When MySpace and LinkedIn came on the scene in 2003, and Facebook soon after in 2004, social media was invented. Twitter and its 140 character messages was a few years later, launching in 2006. Social media is a fun way to share updates, photos, and interesting information with individuals, organizations, and groups. It is a way to stay in touch with family and friends with minimal effort—no conversations needed— and a way to stay connected in business. Thanks to Four-square, we can even let people know where we are located at all times so they can meet us. Cojourneo makes it possible for us to take video workshops powered by human connection, which help us embark on our personal journeys; and provides technology to have direct contact with the workshop guide and collaborate with our fellow participants—all via real-time video. By the time this book is published, there will probably be 10 more social media platforms designed to do things yet to be imagined.

Social media can be a lot of fun, helping us to stay in touch with many more people than we possibly could with traditional letters or even by phone. It can also be very helpful to one's career, and it provides new marketing/promotion channels for business. You can choose to leverage social media as part of your marketing strategy to build your personal brand and your entourage.

You can use your entire digital ecosystem, including a blog, website, Twitter, and social media profiles, as a way for people to find and connect with you, and you with them, online. Social media is not only on our computers, iPads, and tablets, but now it also accessible on a smartphone. With this development, we can choose to monitor our multiple communications channels, no matter where we are, and on a moment's notice. Some people are rarely unconnected.

How Social Media Is Changing How People Relate

Only a few months ago, a group of students got on a crosstown bus I was riding. In the past, noise, laughter, and raw energy pervaded the atmosphere when a group of students came on board. This time it was a whole new experience for me. The students ran up the steps of the bus and quickly and quietly found seats, barely speaking to each other. I looked over the shoulder of the girl sitting next to me.

It appeared that she and the group were texting each other rather than speaking to each other. I was happy for the quiet but disturbed by the lack of fun and live connection going on among them.

What is going on? Cell phones, smartphones, social media, and texting are changing the world. With this change, we are losing our ability to make face-to-face connections, build relationships, and have interesting conversations.

I ride a commuter train almost every day. Five years ago, I'd get on the train, and people would be sharing engaging conversations about the news, politics, and family challenges. Some of them even played a lively game of cards. Today, about 50 percent of the riders are looking intently at their tiny devices, hitting buttons, and staring at mini-screens, expectantly waiting for information. There's no emotion. There's no fun. There's no conversation. The other 50 percent are talking into hands-free headsets and appear to be talking to themselves or some invisible people. Sometimes, I'm surrounded by people engaged in multiple conversations on their phones. I can barely think, let alone read my iPad or Kindle. An interesting study at Cornell University backs this up. It revealed that our brains are unable to tune out half a conversation, suggesting that a "halfalogue" is more annoying and distracting than a dialogue between two people.

I say bravo to Skype, Gmail, and Internet companies like Cojourneo that enable us to see each other and speak to each other on video across the world. However, video communication is not nearly as powerful as sitting down next to each other over a cup of coffee, a glass of wine, or lunch, but at least you can see a person's expression. Internet video serves as a valuable substitute for many both personally and professionally due to the high cost of travel and our tight schedules. However, it takes a face-to-face meeting to feel the sincerity, activate intuition, and build real trust.

One other downside of social media, e-mail, and texting (referred to as SET) is that they often are addictive. Thanks to our mobile devices, SET is served up on one platter wherever we are—crossing the street, in the car, even in bed—within nanoseconds. Many of us can't stop checking, reading, and responding. It distracts us from focusing on our work, it interrupts our sleep, and worse yet, it causes accidents, which is why some states are outlawing texting as well as cell-phone conversations while driving. It's almost as dangerous as driving under the influence. In my opinion, it's dangerous to even cross the street while talking on the phone or texting, and, perhaps, that should be outlawed as well.

The long-term effects of SET and the damage it can cause to our careers, our families and our relationships must be considered. It has replaced much of our face-to-face communications. Many people, especially those who work primarily at their desks, never get up, never get out, and rarely build REAL relationships with people. When I say REAL, I'm talking about the kind of relationships that come from face-to-face, in-person contact.

Now don't get me wrong. I use social media, e-mail, and texting. All three serve a valuable purpose, but they do not replace meeting face-to-face to build trust, to connect on a personal level, and to get to know the authentic person. A deeper connection occurs when you meet with someone live and in person. This just does not happen when using social media or e-mail.

To truly build relationships that will benefit your career and your life, you must take time over coffee or a meal to build your connection. You can introduce yourselves to each other over e-mail. You can find people you have lost touch with on LinkedIn or on Facebook. You can follow the ramblings of people from your past or even your future on Twitter. However, to get to know each other and to discover how you can collaborate to support each other's success, the best method is still the face-to-face way.

How Silicon Valley Entrepreneurs Connect

Take a lesson from the creators of social media. How do they connect with each other? How do they open doors to opportunities? How do they find jobs and build their careers?

An article in the *New York Times*, "A Circle of Tech: Collect Payout, Do a Start-Up" (Somini Sengupta, May 9, 2012), tells it all. The article is about how founders and former employees of some of the biggest Silicon Valley companies, like Facebook, PayPal, and LinkedIn, take their big earnings and acquired knowledge and launch startups that become the next big companies like Instagram, Quora, Asana, and Cove.

The teams that came together to form these social media enterprises did not meet online. They may create social media for us to use, but when it comes to their own connections, they prefer live. They connect on the job, at parties, at business association meetings, and through

97

personal introductions from their entourage. They sit down face-to-face to get to know each other better. The result is powerful relationships that help them launch their next business. They all have entourages.

Ruchi Sanghvi, the first female engineer at Facebook, launched a technology infrastructure company called Cove, and sold it to Dropbox. In the *New York Times* article I previously referenced, she attributes her success to the people around her. Ruchi says, "It's extremely useful to have that network, not just for tangible things like funding and talent but also [for] emotional support . . . just having those friends has been incredibly important."

Bill Tai, a veteran investor, shares, "The social fabric of Silicon Valley is a dense set of overlapping spider webs, meaning everyone is connected." Bill is not talking about being connected on social media; he's talking about a chain of connections and connectors, born through sit-downs and live conversations. Their solar systems overlap.

Where do Silicon Valley entrepreneurs meet with investors and other colleagues? They share ideas at breakfast at their favorite spots—Buck's in Woodside, Il Fornaio and Hobee's in Palo Alto. They often spend the morning meeting with various people, making face-to-face connections. That's probably one reason the economy is thriving in Silicon Valley.

How to Use Social Media to Recruit Your Entourage

There is a place for social media. It can be a helpful tool. To truly succeed, however, face-to-face communications are required. Personal relationships are built by learning about each other's visions, goals, and challenges, and by building trust.

There are four ways to use social media as a valuable tool to achieve your goals.

1. **Social media is a great way to reconnect with people with whom you have lost touch**. Because you are always building your entourage, it's never too late to recruit people whom you respect and admire from your past. No, I'm not talking about the high school quarterback or the homecoming queen, though in some cases they might be appropriate. I'm talking about people from college, grad school, from past employers or members of clubs, whom you used to know and respect. Thanks to social media, especially LinkedIn, you can find them again. Look them up. What are they doing? Do you have something in common with them? Are they up to something big? Do they work for a company you would like to do business with?

   Reconnect with them through social media and, where appropriate, use that as a springboard to connect over the phone or in person. Send them a direct message to meet for coffee. They just might be someone who should be in your entourage. If not, nothing ventured, nothing gained. You never know. It's fun to catch up and find out how people's careers have developed. Reminisce and get reconnected to your past.

2. **If your social media connections are less than 100, it's time to grow them**. For social media to be effective, it's important to have an audience. If you have less than 100 followers on Twitter, friends on Facebook, connections on LinkedIn and the like, take the time to grow your list. First, make sure you're active and update your profile information and be sure to include your vision. Then, invest a few hours in searching for people at companies based in your area or city that sound interesting, people you'd like to meet. Reach out to them to connect with you. See whom your real friends and colleagues are connected to, and invite the appropriate people to connect with you, too. You can do the same thing with Twitter.

   Follow more people that have interesting tweets that fit with your vision. Twitter etiquette urges them to follow you back. Then, you can direct tweet them. Share valuable content through Twitter. It should be content related to your goals. Start building your online connections. Remember, don't sell directly on social media. Provide information, content, or let people know about interesting events. Start expanding your social-media connections.

3. **Meet with people who are on your social media lists of connections or friends**. I recommend this as a secondary tactic to grow your entourage. As I mentioned earlier, first reach out to family, friends, professionals in your life and community, members of organizations, and past connections on your

contact list. When you have finished pursuing those opportunities, it's time to use social media.

Go through your list of connections, followers, or friends on LinkedIn, Twitter, Facebook, or other social media. Read their profiles, as well as your shared connections. See if you have connections or friends in common. If their background reveals commonality with your vision and goals, then take it to the next step, and do an online search and see what you can learn about them on the web in articles, blogs, websites, and so forth.

You may find a lot about the person or maybe not much at all. That in itself tells you something. If this expanded search reveals more commonality, then reach out to them through LinkedIn (or e-mail if you can get their e-mail address) and invite them to schedule a time to talk on the phone. Be sure to explain why you believe it is worth this person's time to speak to you. Share what you have in common and say that you'd like to explore how you can support each other. If the phone conversation goes well and you have things in common, the face-to-face meeting comes next. Invite the person to have coffee or a Skype call if he or she is in a different city.

Now you are on your way. Do the same thing by reaching out to people who are members of the same LinkedIn groups as you are. Make sure you are a member of groups that share your vision or are related to your business or career. If you're not, then join them. Contribute to the group so that

Linking Out with Social Media

people see your name flashing by sharing articles, comments, and videos. Once you've made an impression, then link out to those in the group with whom it makes sense to connect.

4. **Be visible: share your vision on social media**. Many people won't speak to you until they have looked you up on the Internet. They want to know as much as possible about you before they commit to talk or meet. Yes, they are judging you and asking themselves, "Is it worth my time to connect with this person?" This is true of potential employers, customers, investors, clients, or people you just met at a meeting or party. You owe it to yourself to have a big presence on the Internet and in social media.

One of the most important adjuncts to business or any career today is to be visible on the Internet. Social media is an important tool to help you stand out and apart from everyone else. It is a billboard of our credentials. There's a growing belief that you don't exist, if you can't be found on social media.

Social Media Tips to Communicate Your Personal Brand and Vision

This notion of being visible is an important thread throughout this book. The same applies to social media. Here are some tips to increase your online visibility.

- **Start by doing an Internet search on yourself**. What have you found? Whatever you see is what others find. Your Internet footprint should tell a story and present a story of what you stand for today. If you are not satisfied by what you see, it's time to take action.

Is it difficult to find you when you use a search engine, or when you do a search on any of the social networks? It could be because several people share your first and last name. You might want to consider adding a middle initial to distinguish yourself and make it easier for others to find you. If you choose to do that, be sure you use that middle initial on all your postings, your website, resumé, and everywhere you can.

If you have an uncommon nickname, use it to differentiate yourself. My daughter now uses her nickname, Sari, on everything—her blog, website, social media profiles, resumé—so that she is distinguishable online from the many people that share her first and last name. Now people can find her quickly.

- **Check out your profile on LinkedIn, Facebook, Twitter, and so on**. Are they all up to date? Take advantage of the opportunity to write a summary of your career on LinkedIn. Use the LinkedIn summary to communicate your personal brand. Be sure to incorporate your vision in the summary, so people understand what you stand for, where you are headed. Share anything that differentiates you and expresses your passion. Your LinkedIn profile could be the most visible thing on the web. If you are not yet participating, it's time to get started. If you have time for only one platform, I recommend LinkedIn.

- **Select the right path in social media**. The relevancy of the social network or platform for you depends on your goals. Perhaps one form of media will suit your career or business over another. If you are a professional in any field or you are a business owner, LinkedIn should be part of your social media presence. By joining LinkedIn groups, you can narrow and focus your online relationships to people in your industry or profession. If you have a retail business or a nonprofit, Facebook is a great way to reach out and communicate and expand your audience. There are many smaller social networks specific to a particular industry where you can connect, converse, and be profiled. For instance, if you are in the advertising or media industry, MediaBistro.com is a great place to connect and upgrade your skills. If you are in human resources, then consider HR.com, among others. Whatever your field, you can find an online community, as well as a live community to connect with, just do an online search with Google, Yahoo, or Bing.

- **Start a personal website or blog**. Think of yourself as a brand. You can have your own website, and should, especially if you have your own business, projects, or even activities related to your passion. Include your portfolio of work, writing samples, or other important information on your site. Blogging is a great way to communicate with your entourage and grow it. Blogging helps you establish your name as a brand. Just like commercial brands, it helps your career by shouting your personal brand from the rooftop. In today's world, the rooftop is the Internet and social media.

There are many resources that provide the tools and templates to create your own website or blog at no cost to you. Platforms like WordPress, Jimdo, tumblr, and Yola offer basic website designs and blog landing pages free with minimal cost for upgrades providing more options and features. Then, use social media to link to your latest blog posts.

- **Get your message out**. Writing about your passion, your work, your favorite leisure activities, or even your life, is the best way to get the message out about who you are. Blog about what's important to you and what you believe people will be interested in about you. One rule of blogging: be authentic. If you are faking, people will find out. Remember, that whatever you write is everywhere, so be cautious with personal information. Getting your blog into the blogosphere is not difficult. Use social media to link to your latest blog posts.

- **Ramp up your professional and nonprofit activities**. When you join a professional association, volunteer to be on a committee, chair that committee, or ultimately become an officer for the organization, your visibility on the web increases big time. Your name appears on the organization's website, in press releases and announcements, and suddenly you become more important when someone does a search. The more you do, the more visibility you will have on the web. You can even send out your own virtual press release about your nonprofit activities, speaking engagements, and other involvements that relate to your career. Check out Freepressrelease .com and other resources to get the message out.

- **Be sure to link all these tools together**. Mention all your Internet and social media tools on your website. Link your blog and Twitter postings to your Facebook and LinkedIn. You might even design a newsletter to send out to your list of contacts. Make use of all the services on Constant Contact, MailChimp, FeedBurner, and the like. Even Gmail offers free resources that can help you get your message out.

- **Connect with others in online groups**. Begin building online relationships by participating in online groups related to your business or career, like those on LinkedIn and industry-specific social networks. You can build a presence by sharing articles, videos, and comments. When you notice the same people are sharing, it provides an opportunity for you to reach out and take the conversation offline. You never know what opportunity this could provide. If you are a regular reader of the *Huffington Post* and other online media, you can add your comments to the blogs.

On Cojourneo you can participate in video discussions with a small group of people who are taking a multisession online workshop with you. Everyone completes a profile, so it provides an opportunity to build relationships with people who share a common goal. There are many interesting opportunities for you to connect and talk to others online.

- **Monitor and schedule your brand**. If you want to find out your presence on the web there are many tools that you can easily implement. Google Alerts will enable you to monitor whenever your name or your company appears on the Internet, and it's free. Most of the e-mail marketing companies, like Constant Contact, also offer customer relationship management (CRM) tools and analytics, and Nutshell Mail gives you regular reports on your social-media activity, integrating messages from your connections all in one place, to save you time. Other handy tools include Sprout Social, Monitter for Twitter, Google Analytics, Wildfire, and Klout. You should also consider using tools like HootSuite, Twuffer, and CoTweet for all kinds of social-media features, including scheduling tweets, mentions, and the like, so you can plan in advance and not be tied down to daily social-media work.

Your Brand and Connections Grow with Social Media

Can you imagine if you do all these things? Social media and the Internet are incredibly helpful in communicating your vision and your billboard, and they can get the word out about you to the people you want to reach. Now that you have all that attention, use it to build the in-person relationship. Social media is a great way to keep your brand in front of people. It takes sitting down together for you to ask people how you can support them. After you do, they will surely support you in accomplishing your goals.

That means meeting them in person, if they are based in your area, or scheduling a Skype or phone conversation, if they are across the country, across your state, or on the other side of the world. I recommend you use Skype. It's the closest thing to meeting in person, and seeing each other helps to build the relationship.

LINK NOW: Five Tactics to Transform Social-Media Contacts into Real-World Connections

1. Make it a practice of sending an invitation to connect online immediately after you have met someone in person at a meeting, networking event, or social event.

2. Identify all online friends or connections that are in similar or related careers, or professions. Continue to grow your connections by asking your present social-media contacts for introductions to new people that you would like to meet or that you notice on LinkedIn or on other social media. This is one way to grow your contacts.

3. Join more groups that are relevant to your business. Then nurture your online individual and group relationships by commenting more, and by sending them relevant links to articles, videos, and websites. When possible, send links to them directly. Also, read their posts, articles, and so forth so you can comment on them and continue to build your online relationship in two directions.

---

4. Once you feel that you've built a connection, reach out to those with whom you see commonality. Suggest meeting or scheduling a call to uncover how you can support each other and make mutual introductions.

5. Follow the Rules of Engagement in Chapter 4 to connect and possibly engage others as members of your entourage.

7

Launching or Reigniting Your Career

Never tell a young person that anything cannot be done.
God may have been waiting centuries for someone ignorant
enough of the impossible to do that very thing.

—John Andrew Holmes

A New Career Model

Sheryl Sandberg, COO of Facebook, gave the commencement address to the Harvard Business School 2012 graduating class and said, "Careers are not a ladder; they're a jungle gym. . . . Move sideways, move down, move on, move off . . . don't expect a direct climb." Sheryl Sandberg's speech helps to dispel the myth that when we are on our career path, we must always move straight up the ladder to the top.

Most of us have a picture of what we believe our career should look like. What happens if we need to get off the jungle gym for a while due to other responsibilities in our life or a desire to pursue a new career? What happens if we get pushed?

Another career myth is that the career process can only be developed and grown by the person whose career it is. In other words, you have to do it by yourself. Create a great resumé, work hard, and you will be rewarded. That may have been true 15 years ago, but no longer.

Today, you need the support of others in order to move your career in the direction you desire. Even on a jungle gym, staying in motion requires an entourage to help you keep your balance and take new steps in every direction. It doesn't matter if you are launching, rebooting, or transitioning into a new career. It doesn't matter whether you are fresh out of college or grad school, returning to the workplace after a hiatus, or reinventing yourself after being downsized or flat out fired. In today's world, with an entourage you will always have support, advice, and connections to get you where you want to go, even 25 years from now.

Even with an entourage, launching and managing a career can become downright frustrating in the midst of a fast-changing world or in a challenging economy. In addition to following the recommendations in this book in the previous chapters, consider these tips to deflect the down days and boost and stimulate your career.

Tips to Survive Career Frustration

- **Take online education courses and workshops**. Coursera, UDEMY, and Cojourneo are courses you can take to update your knowledge and bring you up-to-date on the latest info in your field of choice. Even if your budget is slim and your time is limited, these affordable and free courses can enable you to learn on your own schedule. Employers are surprisingly receptive to the value of online education. Most will perceive you as a highly motivated individual who wants to stay up on the latest trends in your industry. This will also build your confidence and make you conversant on the newest information.

- **Through the process of linking out, identify others who have been through your personal experience and have come out winners**. Seek them out and schedule time to talk to them about what they did to launch their careers, start a business, or transition into a new field. Learning what others have done can help you learn what to do and what not to do.

- **Commit to getting out of your home or office to attend stimulating programs and meetings relevant to your new career**. When you learn new things, you will begin to see new opportunities, plus you can link out. You never know who you will meet.

- **If your computer and social-media skills are poor or nonexistent, remember, you are never too old or too busy to learn them**. Take a course (most communities offer them for nominal fees), an online workshop, or ask younger people in your life to mentor you. Reverse mentoring is an important trend in today's world. Younger people can coach those older on the latest in tech, and older people have years of wisdom to help the newbies.

- **Make a list of your accomplishments every day**. Sometimes we think we are not making progress when, in fact, we are. By keeping a list, you can see what you have done to move forward. On the other hand, if your list is very short, you will realize that you can do more. Use the 'Link Now' lists in this book, and commit to doing a few more things each day. You will feel less frustrated.

- **Consider getting experience through an internship, no matter what your age or situation**. Internships can change a career stalemate and provide a source for knowledge, experience, and entourage support to people of all ages and all career challenges. Read on for the scoop on internships.

The Internship: Not Just for First-Timers

An internship is not just for people in college or recent grads. Internships in your field of interest are an excellent way to get on-the-job experience to launch, relaunch, or transition your career, or start your own enterprise. In addition to experience that will upgrade your resumé, an internship enables you to boost your entourage and build solid connections.

There's a lot of controversy around internships, especially unpaid internships. Some say it is slave labor. I say, you can save yourself years of slavery in a job you hate. In an internship you cannot only discover what you want to do in your career, but also what you don't want to do. An internship is the best way to get experience on your career path when full-time paying jobs in your field are not available to you. If you are not in a position to take a full-time internship, then consider combining a salaried part-time job in a field that brings in a paycheck, which will leave time for a part-time internship in the field that you want to pursue. Any experience, even a few hours a week, will give you a leg up on your career path, and most important, it will give you the chance to start to build your entourage, in your preferred field.

Although it's true that some internships are mostly grunt work, I say, even grunt work can be incredibly valuable. If you are a good listener, you can hear all the conversations of the people around you and learn from them. Do the grunt work with a smile, but then ask to attend meetings, conferences, and so forth, so that you can learn from them. If you've been happily doing the things no one else wants to do and you ask to be involved in projects that interest you, your supervisors will probably be agreeable. Be specific about what you are asking to help with. If you hear a discussion at a meeting about what is needed, offer to assist or do it. Not only are you likely to get more responsibility, but your colleagues will be impressed. Now is the time to begin to look at all the people around you as potential members of your entourage and start treating them as such. They could be the conduits to a full-time paid job in the field of your choice.

Bring positive attention to yourself. Come to work early. Stay late. Show the team that you are really serious about your internship. By staying late, you'll be there when the leaders are still at work. You can drop by their offices and ask if there's anything you can do to help them. Not only can you get a more interesting assignment, but you will also capture their attention.

People want to help the up-and-comers, and they may invite you into their office to chat. That's how relationships begin. One of the most valuable assets of an internship is the people with whom you meet and connect—your entourage. If the internship doesn't lead directly to a job on site, the new people you meet may help you by offering advice and making introductions. Just follow the rules in the earlier chapters, and you will be on your way.

I have had many interns of all ages, from 19 to 60: college students, recent grads, people who have been out of work for two years, people who just got their masters in their fifties and were transitioning into a new career. All of them ended up in jobs they loved after their internship. I became part of their entourage and offered them much of the information in this book. They all succeeded by realizing their goals and working to achieve them.

Transitioning or Reigniting Your Career

Judy was a stay-at-home mom for 20 years. When her children went away to college, she decided to get her masters in market research in an online program. After trying unsuccessfully to get a job for six months, she took an internship with me, which continued for six months. While she was interning, I encouraged her to join a professional research association and get active in the organization. As a volunteer, she met several committee members who had management positions at big companies. After seeing Judy in action,

116

Link Out

welcoming people to association meetings, one of those people hired her as an interim employee. Judy also contacted her cousin, who was the retired editor of a major media company. When he learned what she was doing, he connected her with a former colleague. Judy got a part-time job in the research department. With her resumé building through her internship and part-time jobs, a full-time job in her field was in her near future.

Ann had a career as a marketing coordinator for five years. She interned for me after she was downsized due to the recession and couldn't find a paying position. During her internship she helped with marketing and event management. She met many new people, and was energized by working on new projects and meeting new people. She started networking more and building her entourage. In less than a year of her internship, she achieved a great salaried job as a marketing manager with an influential firm, and her career is flying high.

When you are unemployed, it can be boring and depressing. It colors your attitude, your energy, and your passion. Getting out of the house and learning and connecting with new people in an internship build your confidence and give you a positive attitude, which is essential when you are out there trying to get a job. Which is more productive? Staying home, spending the day sending your resumés out and watching the soaps, or working in an internship, getting experience, making connections? You can still send out your resumés when you get home, but by investing your time in an internship, you add a new position and considerable experience to your resumé.

My student interns, Nerisah, Leigh, Eric, and Erica, were a pleasure to work with most of the time, but at the beginning the lack of skills of a few of them concerned me. All of them, except Erica, were undergrads or grad students. Erica was a recent college graduate. They started off quite green, but they completed their internships looking like shiny, polished red apples. They were literally transformed by the experience. I mentored them and shared insights and tips for getting and keeping a job. Through the internship, they learned important job skills: how to look your supervisor in the eye, instead of looking out the window; learning to take notes when your manager gives you assignments. They honed their social-media, PowerPoint, and telephone skills, and were thrown into situations they never would have encountered, like meeting and greeting A-list speakers and experts. All these experiences built their confidence and skills. All of these interns now hold well-paying, satisfying jobs. I believe their internship experience made all the difference. I urge students to start doing internships early in their college career. The more experience they get during the college years, the more likely it is that they will get a good job upon graduation.

Ask yourself these questions before you pursue an internship:

- What experience and skills do you want to learn?
- Will you have the opportunity to learn those skills as an intern?

- Who will you report to?

- How can you transform your intern experience into a possible career?

The Treasure Map: Discovering the Career of Your Dreams

I have taken many self-actualization courses over the years including Insight Training, Landmark Education, and others. Each of them provided powerful insights that helped me become the person I am today. One of the tools, I learned in an Insight Training workshop was treasure mapping (some call it a vision board).

It's an easy and fun exercise that helps you identify what you want in your life—both material things as well as your career vision. One way to create your own treasure map is to get a pile of old magazines and cut out photos, artwork, and headlines that represent the things that you want in your life, and paste them in an artistic arrangement on a piece of cardboard of any size. I personally like to use a board that is at least 14 inches by 18 inches, but whatever size you choose is fine.

I did my first treasure map when my children were four and seven years old. I had recently left my job as an account supervisor for a public relations agency and had launched my own agency. We had just moved to a new, much bigger home. About three months after moving, my husband lost his job. We had a big mortgage and I had only one client. Things were looking bleak. That's when I created my first treasure map. I cut out magazine photos of a new car—ours was in bad shape—a family on vacation at a beach, a woman sitting at a beautiful desk in a nice office, children happily playing with friends, a man and woman having dinner in a nice restaurant, and a woman in a beautiful workout outfit exercising in a modern gym. I added a photo of my husband and me, looking happily at each other, and a photo of each of the kids. Then I cut out headlines that said, "Building Business for the Future," "Relaxing, Fun Vacationing," "Fit and Happy," "Don't Worry, Be Happy," and "Realize Your Dreams." I pasted everything on the board, matching the headlines to the photos and magazine clips. I looked at it when it was finished and it made me smile.

I put it on my desk at home and looked at it every morning and every night for months. Then, it disappeared. I didn't realize it was missing until one morning, about one year later, my daughter was retrieving a ball behind my desk and she found it. "What's this, Mommy?" my daughter asked. I looked at it and was shocked to discover that I had come into the treasure shown on map. Every treasure pictured or communicated through the headlines on the map had become a reality for me and my family.

I was overcome by happiness and surprise. The map helped me focus on what I wanted to happen and my subconscious went into action. I had grown my business into a successful enterprise. We had bought a new car and gone on vacation with the family. I had hired a personal trainer, and my family was healthy and happy. My husband and I were no longer worried about the future.

It wasn't magic. It was hard work. The map, just like writing one's vision, provided a path and focus to achieve my goals and my vision. Since then, I have created two more treasure maps, and they were also good motivators in moving forward to launch new businesses and make new dreams real.

Have some fun. Create your own treasure map to launch, transition, or reignite your career and your life. Today, you can print things right off the Internet, and you can find or create the words, headlines, symbols, and photos that illustrate what you want your career to look like. Add some personal things, too. You can find the perfect representations on the Internet, on sites like Pinterest, and others. You could actually create your treasure map on Pinterest, but personally, I like to have a free standing board that I can move around with me and put someplace that is always in my view, such as on my desk, on my makeup table, or in the kitchen, wherever it will catch my eye. If you look at your map often, your brain and your energy will move you in that direction. You will find the treasure—a career that you love.

Real Life Career Adventures

The best way to learn how to launch or transition a career is to learn from others' experiences. Here are two such stories that will give you many ideas of what's possible if you are willing and eager. Both stories start during college, include several internships, and each progresses in a unique direction.

Josh's Story

It was fall 2000, my junior year at Penn State in State College, PA. I was majoring in telecommunications and although I didn't go to all my classes every day, I did go to my broadcast sales class. I went because I loved TV and my professor had interesting speakers who shared the inside stories of the industry. At one class, our guest speaker was the general manager of the local TV station in Altoona-Johnstown area. After class, I went up to him and told him I was interested in an internship in broadcast sales at his station. He told me to come up to the station and I could interview for an internship. I figured I would be good at sales because I had been selling my parents since I was eight. I got the sales internship, and even though I did a lot of grunt work, I did it with a smile, knowing I was learning the basics. I read every document that I collated into kits. I learned a lot about selling TV time, listening to all the conversations that the sales guys had with prospects, occasionally accompanying them to meetings. I had to drive two hours round-trip, three times a week to get to the station. It was well worth it.

Before that internship ended, I sent my resumé with a cover letter to CBS Sports in New York City applying for a summer internship in the public-relations department. After two interviews, I got the position. My previous internship gave me some experience to get this one. I spent the summer learning the PR side of sports broadcasting. It was tremendously exciting, even though I managed to break my jaw on a weekend outing. I couldn't speak for half the internship because my jaw was wired shut, but I showed up to work every day and managed to communicate through notes. I even offered to take on extra work. I wanted to prove to my boss that I would not let anything stop me from doing my best. Back at Penn State, the following semester, I took another communications class and I got to know my professor pretty well. I always stayed after class to meet the speakers. This professor introduced me to the general manager of a local radio station. I asked him a few questions and then asked if there were any openings at the station. Much to my surprise, he invited me to interview for a full-time job as a paid account executive after speaking to my former boss at the Altoona TV station. I arranged my schedule so that I could work in the day and take my classes at night. I realized that I loved sales and much preferred it to PR. Graduation was approaching, so with a recommendation from my boss at CBS Sports where I had my summer internship, I was able to get an interview back at CBS in New York City for the sales-management-training program. With two internships under my belt and a full-time job selling radio time in State College, I had much more experience than most of those applying for the program. I got in.

After graduating from the sales-management-training program, which was like getting an MBA in sales, I was assigned as a sales account executive at the

(continued)

(*continued*)

Philadelphia CBS affiliate. All this time, I kept in touch with all my former bosses, and the coworkers I had met. I had created the beginning of my entourage. This was about the time that the Internet was really coming up strong. The bubble had burst and Internet companies that were still around were doing really well. I was enamored by the Internet and saw it as the future. After a year in Philly, one of my former coworkers from CBS, who had taken a job at a hot digital company, suggested I apply for an opening. I got the job. In fact, within a short time, I became the director of sales. One connection led to another connection, and since that first job in digital sales, I've worked at two different companies, each larger than the previous one, and each time my title and salary has increased. I am now vice president of sales for a major digital company in sports. I can honestly say I love my work. I'm living my passion for sports and sales.

I owe it all to building solid relationships starting in college and continuing through my career—that, plus working hard, taking the initiative, stepping outside my comfort zone, assessing the company's needs, and putting together a plan and presenting it to my boss, even if he didn't ask me to do so. I learned that being a go-getter pays off. You have to stay connected to people and ask for what you want. At the same time, I'm always looking for ways to help other people, too. I've helped many people in my entourage get jobs and given them advice. I love how it feels to help other people succeed.

Sara's Story

Since I was 13, I always knew I wanted a career in art, but there are many different art-related careers. I didn't know what direction I should take. I loved sketching fashion designs and even sewed clothes for my fashion dolls. Before I started college, I had my first internship, which my Mom helped me get. It was at a fashion dress company. One of the good things about internships is that often they help you find out what you don't want to do. After that internship, I knew the fashion industry was not for me. During college in New York City, I had internships at Sony Music, *Time Out* magazine, where I wrote about art shows, and later at a Soho art gallery. I got them through the career center at my college, School of Visual Arts. Did I find my passion at any of these three companies? No, no, and no.

After graduating, I moved to Pittsburgh and got a job at an art museum. My internships gave me the experience to get a paying job. Here I learned that I could eliminate museum work from my list of careers. So far, I was striking out on all the careers in the arts I tried. I returned to New York City and got a job as a design assistant in home accessories at ABC Carpet, one of the leading home stores in the country. I liked the work, but the stress was more than I could handle. I encountered the same stressful environment at my next job at an architectural/interior-design firm, where I worked as materials librarian and design assistant. Neither of these jobs was suitable to my personality, but I learned a

(*continued*)

(*continued*)

lot about what I loved to do. In my last job, I was in charge of educating the designers about the newest materials and products. I loved the education part of the job and enjoyed training the interns. I discovered that I liked teaching.

Once I realized that teaching might be right for me, I started volunteering in my spare time, testing out my interest in an art-education career. After work and on weekends, I spent my time reading to disadvantaged children. I became an arts mentor, bringing art projects into classrooms without a formal arts curriculum. I realized I loved this. It was the first time I wasn't struggling in my career. Teaching seemed to come natural to me. I was the happiest I had ever been. By researching, I discovered that I needed to get my masters, so I decided to go back to the School of Visual Arts (where I got my BA) to get my MAT. After graduating, I quickly got a job as a full-time substitute teacher, teaching art to K-6 grades in a good public school. When I completed that, I got a full-time job as the art educator at a leading charter school.

Throughout my many careers, connections have always played an important role. I realize now that I have built a solid entourage in the art and teaching worlds. I really work at staying in touch with my professors, educators, and artists. Throughout my career I have pursued my love of pottery, working regularly at a studio on the weekends. There I met other potters and teachers, and we stay in touch. I introduced one of my pottery friends to a School of Visual Arts (SVA) friend, who works at the

Museum of Art and Design. Through that connection, my pottery friend became an artist in residence at the museum. He introduced me to a school where I became a visiting artist. We all look out for each other and help each other find opportunities.

I am absolutely crazy about immediately sending handwritten thank-you notes to people who have made introductions and helped me. I keep a list of everyone who has supported me during the year, and then I create handmade artistic holiday greetings for each of them. I want them to know how much I appreciate them, and by sending them the handmade cards, I remind them of my artistic talent. That's one way I distinguish myself from others. In addition, I have a blog in which I feature interesting artwork from shows and museums that I send out to my list. I also have a website that features my artwork. Being a working artist is important to me and is what makes me unique as a teacher.

Although these stories are about Millennials, the strategy and tools they used to succeed in their careers are the same for any age. Everyone has a story, and our stories continue to develop as our careers develop. Some people have a vision for their career early on, as Josh did. For others, it may take longer, like Sara.

Some people have multiple careers, as their lives transition along with their passions. When they have an entourage, they have constant support no matter what new direction they are headed.

Debra Duneier's Story

I've had several careers. I started in the wholesale jewelry and gem business. When my children were born, I took time off to dedicate myself to being a full-time mom. Once my children were in preschool, I had the desire to get back to a career, but I wasn't interested in returning to the jewelry business, which would have required 40-hour weeks.

I maintained my relationships in the jewelry industry, and in conversation with my connections, I realized that there was a need for a dependable, high-end gift service. So I decided to launch a corporate gift service to fill that need. I loved discovering interesting, beautiful items and creating themed gift baskets and packages for every occasion. I combined my strengths as a designer and marketer to create a thriving business. Suddenly my life changed again. This time it was divorce. I gave up the big house and moved to a big city. Not the place for a business that required maximum space for production and storage.

A new career was calling me. I got my license as a real estate broker and, again, just as I turned the corner to building a prospering business, the recession hit. I had a strong interest in feng shui and had become a feng shui master while I was still in the real estate business. I began offering my real estate clients guidance in feng shui to help them differentiate their properties and move the sale of their homes along. This was all happening as the green movement was growing, which seemed to be another extension of the merger of real estate with feng shui. My intuition and love for all things green and natural lead me to pursue a Leadership in Energy and Environmental Design (LEED) certification in the green industry, which was no easy task. After integrating intense study with my real estate business, it culminated in my launching EcoChi, a new company blending feng shui, green and sustainability and environment psychology. Today, my business, along with my book *EcoChi: Designing the Human Experience*, reflects the integration of several of my past careers. I work with real estate developers and contractors bringing EcoChi into their properties to create a healthier, stress-free, more productive environment for their employees, clients, and customers. Between my various careers, I always linked out, building an entourage of supporters who helped me transition from one business to another. Another constant was my desire to always help others in their careers. It is this mutual support that I believe enabled me to continue to develop my businesses.

Changing and establishing a new career is not an easy process, but it is always worth it. Some people have one passion that is consistent throughout their lives. Others, like Debra, have several passions that evolve as their careers do. The sooner you discover your passion or what drives you, the sooner you can create a vision for your career. Once you have your vision, you can build relationships that will lead you to your own entourage—an entourage of people who will support you in launching and growing your career, while you do the same for them.

LINK NOW: Five Tactics to Find a Job, Start a Business, or Get Going Again

1. If necessary, be willing to work without or for minimal pay, and do an internship or volunteer work for an association or nonprofit to get experience in a field for which you want to pursue, launch, or restart your career.

2. Get knowledge about the career to which you aspire by taking courses in higher education or online learning and workshops. Be sure to connect with new people while you are learning.

3. Participate in industry associations in order to connect with people who can mentor you and be part of your network or entourage to get advice and open doors.

4. Step out of your comfort zone and be courageous. Talk to people and try new things that may enable you to live your passion and your vision.

5. Use affirmations, treasure maps, and positive thinking to keep you on track to realize your desire to launch, relaunch, or reignite your career.

8

Grow Your Business and Your Sales by Linking Out

N o matter what your job or line of work, the skills you gain by reading this book will help you reach your goals. You are ready to put link out into practice, and when you do, you will take giant steps. You now know how to build your personal brand by developing your vision, and communicating it to the people you meet. You have learned how to reach out and build relationships with people in various circles of influence in your solar system, even people whom you admire but whom are not yet within your reach. You have learned how to engage and build trust through communications tactics, conversation tactics, and collaboration tactics. You have sharpened your etiquette skills and learned new ways of using social media. These skills can revolutionize your business, career, and day-to-day work.

Link out skills are particularly necessary when you are in sales or business development. This is true whether you work for a small business, a corporation, a nonprofit, or your own enterprise or consulting firm. The link out strategy will play an important role in achieving your sales goals.

To close a sale, you must also have a good product or service that matches the customer's needs as well as a track record and a good presentation to tell your story.

However, no matter how good your product or presentation, you won't get the sale if you can't get your foot in the door in the first place. This is why linking out makes all the difference. Not only can members of your entourage open previously closed doors, but with their endorsement you are welcomed with open arms and a predisposed desire to do business with you.

If you are in the nonprofit world, linking out is a valuable strategy for fundraising. Corporate leaders are sought to serve on nonprofit boards mostly because of their entourages—often bearing deep pockets and a willingness to support each other's causes. Executive directors are hired because of their contacts.

Sales and business-development professionals follow the same link out strategy presented in earlier chapters with a few adaptations. If you are in the business of sales, then pay attention to these differences:

- Define your vision with a focus on business goals, rather than your personal goals.

- Take advantage of the marketing power of the company or nonprofit you represent.

- Create marketing opportunities by promoting yourself as an expert or conduit to information or education related to your business—but never be commercial—never sell.

Without sales and business-development professionals (sometimes called account executives or representatives, among other titles), there is no business. They are the heart and soul of an organization; they are responsible for the growth of the business. Without trained, successful salespeople, a business becomes stagnant—no new customers and no happy repeat customers. A company will lose its energy and reason for being if new avenues to reach new customers are not explored. Business development is a term often used to (1) find new customers; (2) identify new markets with new customers; or (3) arrange alliances, deals, or partnerships that result in new customers. The end game in sales and business development is always the same: new customers.

Business-Development Vision

To attract business, start with a different kind of vision statement: a business-development vision.

The business-development vision communicates your commitment and passion for what you are selling. Begin to formulate this vision by considering why you are selling for a particular company or, if you are a business owner, why you created your business. In the case of a nonprofit, think about the difference you can make by raising funds.

When you link your vision to what you are selling, the listener clearly understands your personal commitment behind the product or service.

To help you begin to create your business-development vision, answer the following questions:

- Why did you choose to work for the company you represent or, if you own the business, why did you start the company?
- What makes you feel proud of what you do?
- What value do you bring to your customer's life? In the case of a business-to-business product or service, what value do you bring to your customer's business?
- How does your connection to the customer make you feel?
- What more could you do to help your customer, which would leave you more fulfilled?

After completing the answers to these questions, go back to Chapter 2 and follow the suggestions in Part 2 of the Personal Vision Quiz and in Your Personal Billboard.

Here's an *example* of a business-development vision statement prepared by a financial adviser who was targeting professional women as clients:

I am committed to helping professional women become financially self-sufficient so that they can realize their dreams. I do this by providing them with the financial education they need to ensure their future.

In this vision statement, she specifically shares what makes her proud of what she does and the value she brings to her customer. This vision statement is helpful in attracting an entourage (and ultimately a customer), because she is no longer only selling financial products but she has a bigger vision of making a difference in the world and helping her clients.

Being able to connect your vision to a larger framework or a long-term goal is an important way to build both positive buzz and loyalty.

Your Entourage: A Source for Referrals

Once you have created your vision statement, share it in a natural and comfortable way with your entourage. When you are inspired by your vision, most likely you will inspire your entourage, too. You may not even have to ask them for referrals. Members of your entourage may be so inspired that they suggest people they know who would benefit from your product or service. If they don't spontaneously make suggestions, it is fine for you to ask them. After all, you've already taken the time to build a trusted relationship with them. They are in your entourage and you are both helping each other. When asking for suggestions, there are a couple of ways you can approach the situation.

Here are a few conversation openers that can make you more comfortable asking for referrals:

- Share a story about how your product or service is making a difference in someone's life or business, and then let your entourage know that you are looking for more people/companies whom you can help.

- Ask your entourage about their goals for the year. Listen carefully and suggest ideas or refer them to people who may help them to reach those goals. Then tell them one of your goals is to increase your business by a certain amount. It's perfectly appropriate to let them know what would be an ideal customer for you, and then ask if they know of anyone who fits that description.

- Let them know that your business grows mostly through word of mouth. Then ask if they can think of anyone who would benefit from what you do or offer. If you have a specific connection you would like to make, ask them if they know that person or company. If they do, then ask if they would feel comfortable making an introduction.

- Always ask about what's new with them and their companies or careers first. If you are in the service business, this opens the door for you to tell them about some projects you have completed. Then you can tell them that, with the completion of those projects, you finally have time to provide your services to more clients, and you wonder if they know of anyone (or any companies) that could benefit from your services.

Word-of-mouth referrals are what drive business today. People are most likely to buy a product or use a service if someone they know suggested it.

Referrals are a natural way to infuse a business with new opportunities. Referrals are gained by using the skills you learned earlier in the book to build strong relationships. You'll get referrals when you maintain long-term relationships and people have wonderful things to say about you.

You need to arm people with a microphone to champion you. When you link out and communicate clearly, this process is completely in your power. There are several ways to keep referrals coming in.

- Keep your entourage up to date with positive stories about what you and your company are doing, through a newsletter or periodic e-mail.

- Pepper your conversation, in a natural way, with personal stories of how you are helping your clients. For example, use informal case studies of how customers are benefiting.

- Don't be afraid to toot your own horn, but practice doing it with subtlety, and always ask about and congratulate members of your entourage on their successes.

- Invite them to attend a workshop, a special event, or an online course that you are presenting about your service or product. Tell them you'd like to get their feedback on your presentation. Not only will you get valuable insights, but by the end of the workshop, they'll also have a clear understanding of what you do.

- Never sound like you are selling your entourage. Speak with modesty and humility about your successes.

When others clearly understand your vision, they will be thinking of you, and when they meet someone who can benefit, they will refer them. Be sure to follow the Rules of Engagement and Entourage Etiquette in previous chapters not only with your entourage, but also with any referrals

137

you receive. The communication tactics in the book apply to potential clients and customers as well. Though often these relationships are transactional, it is best not to treat them this way. Treat every communication as a potential entourage member and you'll find that your chain of connections will grow.

As the owner of my own small business, a public relations and marketing firm in the 1990s, I was the CEO, CFO, COO, and chief salesperson. As I shared in previous chapters, linking out was the key strategy to build my company from startup to a million-dollar-plus enterprise. I got the best results from my involvement in groups. There I met many people who became part of my entourage. I learned over the course of several years that I was able to transform most of the referrals, connections, and introductions, which came from my entourage, into clients and customers.

I participated actively in a mastermind group of 15 business owners for more than three years. At each meeting, members shared what was going on in their business and told the group what kinds of referrals they wanted. We each met separately one-on-one to build individual relationships and have a clear understanding of the value we brought to our customers. Several of the people in this group became members of my entourage. Through this process I received referrals to the marketing heads of top companies like Saab Cars and BBC America, both of which became big accounts. I received these referrals by building trusted relationships as a member of this group.

Due to my involvement in another professional association, I built a relationship with an influential banker at a financial institution by offering to brainstorm with him about ideas to open a new branch. My willingness to help him led to several conversations, after which he asked my firm to make a proposal for business.

Thanks to linking out, I gained many other clients, including a major insurance carrier, a fine-jewelry-industry trade show, Platinum Guild International, and American Express OPEN. American Express was a corporate sponsor for the National Association of Women Business Owners, New York City chapter. As president of the chapter, I worked closely with the sponsors to ensure they received value from their sponsorships, and by doing so, I developed a strong relationship with the director of communications of AmEx. As I shared in an earlier chapter, when people see you in action via your volunteer work, you have the opportunity to show them your commitment and effectiveness. This predisposes them to want to do business with you. This is exactly what happened to me. Through the relationship, I understood the company's goals and helped move them toward these goals. After I stepped down as president, I proposed a project to continue to help American Express reach their goal of building awareness among women business owners. My firm was hired and we delivered results. One year later, I again approached them, this time with the opportunity to sponsor Women's Leadership Exchange (WLE), the organization that I had recently cofounded. I carefully crafted a proposal that showed how sponsorship of WLE would continue to build on what had been accomplished. They said yes to the sponsorship. What made this possible was a recommendation from the director of communications who by now was in my entourage. It was a solid relationship that had been built two years earlier and continued to flourish by linking out.

Marketing for Business Development

Chapters 3, 4, 5, and 6 shared valuable marketing tactics that apply to your sales and business development strategies. Here are some additional areas that are particularly relevant when you sit down with a prospect.

Listening and Presentation Skills

The importance of listening skills was emphasized in Chapter 4, and listening is especially critical in sales. When a member of your entourage recommends a possible customer, you need to get to know them just as you would a potential entourage member.

Consider the following:

- People want to do business with others who they trust and feel an affinity to. Get to know them first. Ask questions about their business and their life and listen carefully. Don't expect to make a sale in the first conversation.

- Allow at least three conversations until trust is built and people decide to do business with you. With women, it can take longer.

- Take notes. This shows your prospect that what they are sharing is important to you.

- Learn about your customer's needs, pains, and what is missing so you can address any issues specifically when it's your turn to speak.

- Be a good presenter, a good talker, and a good speaker. Practice, practice, practice.

- Never sell. Instead, educate. How you converse and intertwine your vision into regular conversation is important. Although you can share information about your product or service, don't sell. When presenting your product or service, always share two to three options with your customer. If you don't offer options, they will be forced to speak to a competitor. Everyone wants options.

Build Your Personal Brand to Grow Your Revenue

In Chapter 3, I shared some things, which I said you do *not* have to do to recruit your entourage:

1. You don't have to get up in front of a room and give your elevator pitch.
2. You don't have to give speeches.

Although this remains true when recruiting your entourage for your personal vision, I *encourage you to do them both when you are in business development.* After all, your livelihood is at stake. In sales, you need to put yourself out

141

there. So here are five suggestions to build your visibility in ways not mentioned in earlier chapters:

1. **Get going on your elevator pitch**. Adapt your business-development vision into an elevator pitch. When you are in sales, you need to be prepared to quickly present your business at a moment's notice, so get that elevator pitch ready and have it memorized, and be prepared to present it in front of a group. By the way, your vision statement and your elevator pitch might be almost the same.

2. **Educate your target audience**. I don't mean educate them on the workings of your products or services. Instead, use your expertise to educate people about relevant topics that will expand their knowledge to help them personally or professionally. It is the start of getting them as customers. For instance, if you are a stockbroker, don't educate clients about your company or specific stocks they should buy. Instead, educate them about stock-market strategies, and which ones have been most successful in the last 10 years, according to research. Look for opportunities to educate people about trends, research, and strategies in your particular category. You can educate people through various communication channels: social-media tips, links to articles, blogs, white papers, workshops, webinars, or speaking engagements. Remember, if it looks like you are selling, or sounds like you are selling, then you are selling. Don't sell, educate.

3. **Prep for speaking engagements**. You don't have to speak in front of groups, but if you do, it will give you a huge advantage. Develop several speaking topics that allow you to share your company's expertise without selling. Be the expert so that you can speak as a single speaker or on a panel, or maybe even moderate a panel. All three opportunities will enhance your profile and interest people in who you are, what you do, and what you sell (without selling).

4. **Give added value**. By listening to your prospect or customer, you've learned about their needs and some of their interests and passions, too. When you meet or speak to them, be prepared to invite them to attend something they would enjoy. It might be an upcoming association meeting, a workshop, a game of golf, a social event, or a conference. By extending such an invitation, it shows that you are *not only* interested in them as a customer, but you want to develop a relationship. They will truly appreciate this. You are showing that you care and people want to do business with people that care. You should also consider inviting the entourage member who referred them to you in the first place. You always want to reinforce the relationship with your entourage, and encourage them to continue to send business your way.

5. **Follow up after the sale**. When you close the sale it's not the end of the cycle; it's just the next stage. It takes three times more time and energy to get a

Grow Your Business and Your Sales by Linking Out

new customer than it does to keep an old one. You want to continue this relationship, so that person becomes a customer for life. If you've built a good relationship, then in addition to continuing to buy more goods or services from you, that customer can become a source of referrals. Even better, that customer might become a new member of your entourage. You already know how to make that possible, so go forth and make it happen.

LINK NOW: Five Tactics to Increase Your Sales

1. Write a business-development vision statement and practice it until it rolls off your lips. If it doesn't excite you, work on a new one.

2. Ask your entourage for suggestions and introductions to support you in developing new business.

3. Develop several speaking topics that enable you to present yourself as an expert in your field to educate—not sell—your target audience.

4. Practice speaking in front of a group by offering to speak free at a few small events or create your own event in a conference room or in a private room of a restaurant.

5. Check in with all your current and target customers. See how they are doing and consider inviting them to a local event.

9

Clear the Accountability Hurdle and Grow Your Entourage

Accountability breeds response-ability.

—Stephen R. Covey

T he word *accountability* is usually associated with the corporate and financial worlds, as well as politics. The board of directors is accountable to the stockholders. Members of Congress are accountable to the citizens who elected them. Leaders are accountable to their constituents, their community or whomever they report to.

As the leader of your life, you are accountable to yourself.

Accountability means being held responsible for your actions and decisions. If you have an entourage, you are accountable in another way. Should you fail to take advantage of the introductions and connections your entourage makes on your behalf, they will surely be disappointed and will quickly stop functioning effectively—no more introductions, no more endorsements, and no free advice. If you take advantage of the introductions, but you fail to inform your entourage of the results, they will have no way of knowing that you took action. Again, your entourage will no longer be responsive, plus you'll endanger your reputation.

The bottom line is that you need to contact the connections that are forged for you by your entourage. If you are not going to do so, then let your entourage know why you are not contacting them. You may have good reason – your plans or goals have changed, you have a family emergency, etc. Communication is everything: always keep your entourage in the loop.

Some of us are outstanding at being accountable to others, but we fail to be accountable to ourselves. Many of us are great at soaking up the knowledge we read in books and articles or learn in webinars and workshops, but how often do we move that information into action, applying it to our life? We certainly have the best intentions, but life gets in the way.

How to Be Accountable to Others

Building a network of long-term connections is the critical strategy for business and personal development. Your network will help you build visibility and credibility and being accountable to others is at the core of this strategy. Do what you say you are going to. Do it within a reasonable amount of time. Inform people that you have done what you said you were going to do, so they know you did it. If for some reason you can't do it, let them know you can't, so they are not waiting for you to do it. Honor your commitments.

Why is being accountable to others difficult for many people? Maybe it's because they have few role models. How do you feel when someone says they are going to do something and you are waiting and waiting for them to follow through? We may feel hurt, or even angry. It may make us feel unimportant. It certainly doesn't make us feel good about the relationship. As children, when people consistently don't deliver, we get used to it and think it's acceptable not to be accountable. Then we do the same to others.

On the other hand, when people follow through on what they say they are going to do, that's the beginning of a trusted relationship. It gives us confidence in the other person and in ourselves. This is critical in developing a strong relationship. When we do what we say we are going to do, it is likely that the other person will treat us as we have treated them. Sometimes you may overpromise. In your eagerness to help out, you may offer to make an introduction to someone who is too busy or disinterested to meet. If this happens, go back to the original person and apologize. Never make the person who was unable to fulfill the request look bad, just tell the truth. Perhaps there is someone else you know that can be helpful to them or maybe you can help them in another way. Don't worry. It happens.

How does being accountability translate to your entourage?

When someone in your entourage introduces you to a new connection who may lead you to a client, a new job, or produce valuable information, immediately thank them for the introduction. In addition, keep them in the loop about the result of their connection. Sometimes there won't be any result from the contact. Even if it results in nothing, still thank them. In fact, if the person who they recommended doesn't respond, let your source of the introduction know. Before you go back to the source, remember the three-strikes-and-you-are-out rule shared in Chapter 5.

Contact the new connection three times before you give up. People can be busy, traveling, or your e-mail went into spam. After three tries, tell your referrer, that you haven't heard back. Most likely, they will reach out to them again on your behalf. If there's still no connection, it just wasn't meant to be. On the other hand, in most cases you will connect with the new person, and great things may come of it. Make sure your entourage is kept informed.

How to Be Accountable to Yourself

You may find that it is more difficult to be accountable to yourself than to others. If this is true, then perhaps it is because you put yourself at the bottom of the list and make everyone else more important. Making commitments to yourself and then not keeping them is a serious problem. When we do this, we are not respecting our own goals, our missions, and the visions we hold dear. The accountability we have to ourselves is interwoven into accountability to others.

Start each day or each week by setting an intention for what you want to accomplish. Write it down and display it where you can see it throughout the day: on your computer, on your mirror, anywhere that it pops out in your line of vision.

Take responsibility for being accountable to yourself and others by keeping a list. Write down all the people you meet with and keep track of the thank-you notes you send, the follow-up you do, the e-mails or resumés you send out. Be sure to list the people to whom your entourage introduced you. This will help remind you to keep them in the loop on your progress and the results that come from their introduction or advice. By writing it all down, you will see the value of your entourage and how it is making a difference in your life. I have created a Link Out Connections Chart (Table 9.1) that you can use to track your contacts, follow-ups, and so forth.

Also be sure to list the people you are helping. This is an important part of having a collaborative entourage. If we don't track it in black-and-white, sometimes we don't realize how much others are supporting us and how we are helping others. It's important to acknowledge the flow and the results. It's a good reinforcement for continuing to build our entourage.

Overcommitting versus Undercommitting

Some of us are afraid to commit to anything. Some of us commit to too much. This affects our ability to be accountable to others and to ourselves. Which describes you?

Those who take a long time moving into action could fall in either category. If you are an undercommitter, you may have a certain fear of connecting with people. It's kind of like the salesman who never asks for the sale. Sure it's scary, but if you want to achieve your goals, you need to get your courage together and connect with people (or for the salesman,

149

Table 9.1 Link Out Connections Chart

Meeting Date/Time	Contact Name/ Title	Phone/ E-mail	Mailing Address	Date Thank- You Sent	Comments

ask for the sale). Remember the cowardly lion in the *Wizard of Oz?* Eventually, he got his courage together and went for it. If you want to realize your vision, fight through the fear, and ask for the meeting.

If you are an overcommitter, you may say you are going to do too much too soon. Therefore, you are left not knowing what to do first. When you are overwhelmed, you may find yourself at a total standstill. When you have a lot on your plate and you have said you will get them all done quickly, you don't know what to do first. You have made it difficult to set priorities. This leaves you doing nothing. I have experienced this personally.

If you are like me, I offer to do too much within an immediate time frame. I truly enjoy contributing and helping others and I don't want to stop, nor should I, since this is how an entourage works. I've trained myself to deal with my overcommittment habits because I don't want my entourage to think I am not accountable. Here's what I do. I find it best not to promise to do things immediately. Instead, when you offer to help, let the person know that your schedule is hectic this week and/or next week, but within two weeks, you will fulfill your commitment. Ask if that works for them.

If they tell me they really need it sooner, than I tell them I will make every effort to get it done on their time schedule. If it is really urgent, I will find the time to meet their request. Sometimes, it means I must renegotiate another commitment I made. Commitments can be changed, but not ignored. As long as you keep the other person in the loop and explain why you need to change the timing, you are still being accountable.

If you are neither an undercommitter nor an overcommitter then—much like Goldilocks' story—you are just right. All you need to do is honor your commitments and pay it forward. Honestly, most of us are *not* just right because we are human, so be sure to look at yourself honestly and make adjustments for where you might fall a little short.

Managing Your Time and Staying Organized

Here are some tips for managing your time and making better use of it.

1. If you are working, set aside at least 30 minutes each day (or one hour every other day) for building your entourage; if you are not working and want to be, spend at least two hours each day on link out activities and you will move forward more quickly.

2. Keep a link out to-do list to stay on top of your progress. Highlight the most important activities, and check them off as you complete them. End the week by looking back on what you accomplished and acknowledging yourself for what you did. If it wasn't a week of accomplishment, don't beat yourself up, just commit to do more the following week.

3. Of course if you are a very busy person, you may find your time limited to plan and execute tactics. We all need to find what works best for us, but for most people it is helpful to wake up a little earlier than usual. If you are a night person, cut short your TV viewing time

---

and use that time to plan your link out tactics and send e-mails. Remember, to maximize the effectiveness of linking out, you need to be consistent.

4. Stay organized with a personal journal to keep your to-do lists, notes from all your conversations with prospective entourage members, and so forth. You may also find the Link Out Connections Chart helpful to track your connections. You'll find an example of the Chart in the book or send an e-mail to leslie@TheLinkOutBook.com to request an Excel version.

5. Keep printed thank-you notes and stamps on hand at all time, so you can get thank-you notes out immediately.

What Can You Expect from Your Entourage

Sometimes people in your entourage may not do what they say they are going to do. In most cases, this is because they are, like many of us, overcommitters or undercommitters. One way to help your entourage along is to remind them, by including it nicely in the thank-you note you send to them after your conversation. It is easily done by adding to the note, something like:

"I really appreciate your offering [specifics of their introduction, advice, etc.]. I look forward to. . . ."

When I receive a thank-you note full of details, I always appreciate it, especially if I had a particularly busy day. Let's face it, sometimes things fall through the cracks.

153

Clear the Accountability Hurdle and Grow Your Entourage

If you find that people in your entourage don't do what they say they are going to do within a week or within the timetable they promised, it's okay for you to gently remind them. I would wait patiently, but then, if it still doesn't happen in two more weeks, one last reminder is okay. After three weeks, if they still don't do it, then it's probably not going to happen. If they fail on more than one commitment, it could be that this person is *not* really in your entourage. Although you may like the person, you can't count on them. Remember, being in an entourage is a two-way street. You need to do what you say you are going to do and so should they.

Just because someone hasn't honored their commitment to you doesn't mean you shouldn't honor your commitment to them. Perhaps you can show them the way to truly build relationships.

Set an Accountability Strategy

When it comes to linking out, strategy is how you get results. To succeed, it is important to set up a plan and manage your time accordingly. Look at your own strengths and weak-nesses in being accountable to others and to yourself. Try to make small improvements each day, but don't be too hard on yourself. It's not always easy to change. Pay attention to what you say to people and whether you overpromise or don't commit enough. Follow the to-do list below to help you become more accountable. Take time at the beginning or end of the day to check in on how you are doing.

Link Out Accountability To-Do List

1. Keep a journal or a folder on your computer to track your progress in linking out and building your entourage.

2. Keep a separate page or document for each person you meet with. Identify them with a capital E if you want them in your entourage; keep a record of what they say they will do for you, what you are doing for them, thank-you notes sent with dates, follow-up, and so forth. This will help you stay on top of everything, without stressing.

3. Always get back to people when you say will, even if they haven't done the same to you.

4. Think about how you can help members of your entourage to accomplish their goals, and then offer to do it.

5. If you are stressed out with too much to do, then don't tell someone you will do something right away. Set a reasonable date that you believe you can meet. Give yourself a few days or a few weeks in the future to meet your commitments. In other words, don't overpromise.

6. Keep members of your entourage informed about your progress. You can do that with a blind copy (bcc) e-mail to all.

7. In your e-mail communications to your entourage, always ask them about themselves and their work. Offer to support them in any way possible.

Clear the Accountability Hurdle and Grow Your Entourage

10

Pay It Forward

Nothing builds self-esteem and confidence like doing good for others.

The final element in the link out process is to pay it forward.

Paying it forward means doing something good for someone else as a response to a good deed done on your behalf. However, when you pay it forward, you don't repay the person who did something for you. Instead, you do something nice for someone else, and the gracious deed is done with no expectation of recognition.

The concept of pay it forward is said to have started as far back as 317 BC in ancient Athens in a play called *The Grouch*. Benjamin Franklin is said to have practiced it back in 1784, and Ralph Waldo Emerson wrote about it in 1841 in his essay "Compensation." Other books have espoused this belief: Robert A. Heinlein's book *Between Planets,* published in 1951, spawned the Heinlein Society, a humanitarian organization; Ray Bradbury's book *Dandelion Wine,* published in 1957, featured it.

Perhaps best known is Catherine Ryan Hyde's novel *Pay it Forward,* published in 2005 and later adapted into a film by the same name, which described pay it forward as an obligation to do three good deeds for others in response to a good deed that one receives. One qualification is that such good deeds should accomplish things that the other person cannot accomplish on their own, spreading geometrically good deeds throughout society at a ratio of three to one. The novel led to a social movement with the impact of making the world a better place.

The Power of Giving

Most of us experience the power of doing good things for others from time to time. We all have such busy lives, we barely have time take care of ourselves. On rare occasions, we stop thinking about what we need to get done for ourselves, in order to do something nice for others. Interestingly, when we take a moment to do something nice, often we are rewarded more than the person upon whom we've bestowed our kindness. Few activities are more energizing and provide such self-satisfaction as doing something thoughtful for another person. It is especially rewarding when they are totally surprised by the gesture.

One day, I dropped my daughter off at the commuter train. I saw two older women looking bewildered and upset. I got out of my car, and asked if I could help them. They told me they had taken the train to make a condolence call to a family who lived in a town about 25 minutes from the station. They expected to find a cab when they got off the train, but there were none around. I knew that there were never cabs at this particular station and were I to call one for them, they would probably be waiting for quite a while in a deserted station. I decided to offer to drive them. At first I was hesitant because I would lose about one hour from a very busy day. The moment I made the decision to help them, I immediately felt happy. I stopped worrying about what I wouldn't get done, and I started feeling good about my decision. Needless to say, my day didn't suffer much without that hour of work, and I was rewarded with a feeling of elation.

You may be surprised to learn, as I was, that a simple act of kindness extended by one human being to another results in an improvement of our immune systems and an increased production of serotonin. Serotonin is a natural neurochemical that is considered the feel-good substance that serves as a pathway for pleasure in the brain. Serotonin has a calming, mood-regulating, and anti-anxiety effect. So when we do good, the serotonin kicks in. This scientific fact gives research-based reason to do good. However, we all know that we get the biggest reward of all when the giving comes from our heart.

Linking Out: A World Vision

Having an entourage puts each of us on the receiving end. An entourage offers us advice, new connections, recommendations, and referrals for clients and customers, too. As I've shared previously throughout this book, the link out process works only when you consider it a two-way street. An entourage not only provides, but it also offers a unique opportunity to give back. Giving back to your entourage and to others outside your entourage is a way for people to collaborate on behalf of one another's success.

The more we link out, the more powerful relationships we will have and the more people we will have in our entourage. Of course, this increases the number of opportunities to make our vision a reality. The other side of the coin is that we also have many more opportunities to do good for others, and help their visions come true. I believe if all of us focus on building our entourages using the link out strategy, we could actually make a shift in the world. Can you imagine if we could reduce stress, anger, hunger, illness, fear, and war and replace it with peace, health, confidence, joy, and love by using the power of giving to each other?

The Pay It Forward Philosophy in Action

A critical part of one's success and happiness is to activate your pay it forward philosophy. This generosity should be toward your entourage, other people in your circle, family, friends, and even strangers you happen to meet. You can activate your pay it forward philosophy by spur-of-the-moment acts of kindness, as well as more premeditated plans to do good for others.

Just as you seek out mentors, offer to mentor someone who needs a person with your experience to help them move on with their career or be better at their job or small business. Bring a group of people together who would benefit from knowing each other, and encourage them to support each other with you leading the group. Offer to share your expertise on a given topic without any expectation of getting business from doing so. For example, work with high school students at a low-income school, by providing job or career advice; offer to take students on a school trip to meet business owners in their area to hear how they started and how they addressed their challenges; or organize an internship program. Think about how you can help your community as part of an organized association or by starting your own association. Doing good will not only help the serotonin kick in, it will also help you realize just how much you have to give to help others, even when your own confidence can use a boost. Paying it forward can shift the energy in the universe. Suddenly you feel optimistic, and your business, career, or sales volume is taking an upward turn.

When we look for opportunities to give back to someone with no expectation of any kind of reward or giveback, we begin to look at the entire world population as part of our entourage. The entourage of the world is all of us making a difference in the lives of whomever we come in contact with, for the common good. When we all join together in this effort, not only will we lead the lives we want, but so will all of those around us, making the world a better place for everyone. Idealist? Yes, indeed.

As we link to each other creating a chain of connections, each of our links connects to another chain of links. As this continues, an exciting discovery emerges. We are all connected. Together we have formed a worldwide entourage of mutual support. I like how that looks. I like how that feels. Do you? I believe the serotonin is kicking in.

About the Author

Leslie Grossman is an award-winning entrepreneur who advises, trains, and speaks on leadership, marketing, and career and business development.

She is founder of Leslie Grossman Leadership, chief connections officer for Cojourneo.com, and serves on the board of Unleashed, an experiential leadership program for middle school girls. As cofounder of Women's Leadership Exchange (WLE), the first national conference series to propel the businesses of women business owners and professionals, she spearheaded the program, reaching more than 65,000 women through more than 100 live events and online programs.

She led Communications/Marketing Action (CMA), an integrated marketing and PR firm, and was actively involved with associations like the National Association of Women Business Owners, where she served as president of the New York City chapter and founding international chair of the national board. Grossman's previous book, *SELLsation! How Companies Can Capture Today's Hottest Market: Women Business Owners and Executives,* was used as a marketing guide and for business development training by companies like Aetna, IBM, Best Buy, American Express OPEN, and IKEA.

Index

171